*F*rom many viewpoints, we are living in the most chaotic time in man's history. Political systems falter, war threatens on every side, shortages loom in every area of need. . . .

From another viewpoint, however, this is the most exciting time in history. A way to success has been laid before us if we will but open our eyes and proceed. My prayer is that this book will make that possible, for even though the times are critical, the possibilities are limitless.

This edition is special just for the friends and partners of the Christian Broadcasting Network. I thank you for standing with us and our worldwide ministry during this time of great challenge and great opportunity.

May God bless you richly.

Pat Robertson

S THE ECRET KINGDOM

PAT ROBERTSON
With BOB SLOSSER

THOMAS NELSON PUBLISHERS
Nashville • Camden • New York

CONTENTS

THE
SECRET KINGDOM

Introduction

The yellow moon hung low over the Atlantic. Two hundred feet from the narrow beach the surf boomed and crashed, streaking white in the crystal moonlight. Beyond the breakers a hundred sea gulls settled for the night, rising and falling in the dark swells.

I turned and looked north. Cape Henry, shadowy under the soft sky, stretched before me, a gathering of sand dunes named after the eldest son of King James I of England. It was utterly peaceful, clutching to itself a history little noticed as the noisy twentieth century raced toward conclusion. For that gentle corner of the Chesapeake Bay's great mouth had been the stage for a small drama of unusual significance to America.

On April 26, 1607, a small band of settlers arrived from England to lay claim to a new world, stepping from their boats into the fine sands of the cape, anxious and weary. Three days later, amazed by this big fresh land, they carefully carried ashore a rough, seven-foot oak cross and plunged it into the sand. As they knelt around it, their spiritual leader, an Anglican clergyman named Robert Hunt, reminded them of the admonition of the British Royal Council, derived from the words of the Holy Scripture: "Every plantation, which my Heavenly Father hath not planted, shall be rooted up."[1]

With face turned toward heaven, the priest then dedicated the vast new land and their future in it to the glory of Almighty God.

Revived, eager, and joyful, these brave pioneers reboarded their tiny ships and sailed around Cape Henry and into the mouth of a river they named in honor of their monarch, James. Before long they sighted an outcropping along the banks that seemed entirely suitable to their immediate needs and on May 3 founded Jamestown, the first permanent English settlement on the North American continent.

Their "plantation" was indeed not "rooted up." From it and later settlements in Massachusetts, Rhode Island, Pennsylvania, New York, and Maryland grew the most prosperous nation in humanity's history. Unparalleled freedom and creativity burst upon the earth.

As I surveyed that historical site and looked eastward at the Atlantic beneath that dazzling moon, I was gripped by the renewed realization that a dread disease had fastened itself upon the lands sending forth our forefathers. As I turned westward toward my car, my mind's eye swept across the huge country that lay before me. And I mourned more deeply because the same sickness was fastening itself upon my land, the new world so sincerely dedicated to God three hundred and seventy-five years ago.

Yes, the disease seemed epidemic throughout the earth. Could it be fatal? Was an "uprooting" to come?

So great are our problems that to think of them as incurable is not unreasonable. Thoughtful men frequently compare the re-

---

[1]Compare Matthew 15:13, KJV.

cent course of Western civilization with the collapse of the ancient Roman Empire. Everywhere scholars, politicians, industrialists, financiers, sociologists, and futurists see grave trouble ahead. Yearningly, they look back to the optimistic beginnings of our country and the whispers seep from their pursed lips, "What went wrong? What happened to the hopes and aspirations of the pioneers? Were their brave struggles in vain?"

The thoughts accruing from many months of reading and meditation poured in upon me that night when I looked upon the Atlantic where the American dream had begun. I, like other concerned persons, seemed to have nothing but questions. Is our nation—our world—faced with collapse? Can we survive? Is our only choice between anarchy and dictatorship? Or is there an alternative?

More than any time in my life, I knew that night that we must urgently seek a third choice. I knew we would have to reach into the invisible world that has been there all along, a world far truer than any civilization in history. We have wasted too much time, decades of delay and doubt.

The challenges of my contemporaries rang in my ears:

Is there truly an invisible world of the spirit?

Is it possible to draw help from that invisible world?

Can there be a new world order?

Yes.

This book comes from convictions about those questions. Its purpose is to foster understanding of the invisible world, better described as an invisible kingdom, the kingdom of God. It has principles. They can be learned.

My recognition of this has come slowly, spanning several years, and is still expanding. First was a prayer for wisdom, spoken quite naively, perhaps in the manner of King David's son Solomon. I desperately wanted to understand—God, the world, the present, the future, the working of things.

Oddly, or so it might seem, my first awareness of the possible answer to that prayer dawned as my interest became fixed on the words of John the Baptist in the early pages of the New Testament: " 'Repent, for the kingdom of heaven is at hand.' "[2]

I was struck by the words "at hand." What did they mean? Eventually my mind recalled similar words of Jesus, spoken the night of His betrayal as Judas approached with his rowdy gang: " '. . . the one who betrays Me is at hand!' "[3]

In this case, the meaning was obvious. Judas had arrived; he was there. John the Baptist, using the same words, had obviously meant the same thing. The kingdom had arrived; it was there, at hand.

This was revolutionary understanding, as simple as it may seem these six or seven years later. I had been instructed to regard our time as the age of the church, and it is that in a very real sense; but John the Baptist and later the Lord Jesus Christ declared the arrival of the kingdom of God. Somehow I had failed to take seriously the fact that the kingdom of God is the central teaching of Jesus. He began His earthly ministry by declaring the arrival of the kingdom,[4] and He ended it by "speaking of the things pertaining to the kingdom of God."[5] Indeed He described such teaching as His ultimate purpose: " 'I must preach the kingdom of God to the other cities also, for I *was sent for this purpose.*' "[6]

That the kingdom of God was at the heart of the Lord's work is obvious, and furthermore He spoke of it as existing then and now, not to arrive at some far-distant time and place. The kingdom of God is in our midst.[7]

---

[2]Matthew 3:2.
[3]Matthew 26:46.
[4]Matthew 4:17.
[5]Acts 1:3, KJV
[6]Luke 4:43.
[7]Luke 17:21.

My constant prayers for wisdom brought additional insight over the weeks, months, and years, and I gradually perceived that Jesus had spoken quite precisely about how this kingdom worked. He was far from theoretical. He actually laid down specific principles, so sweeping that they might be better considered as laws, even at the risk of offending those who cringe at the merest hint of legalism. Jesus quite bluntly said, "If you do this, then this will happen." When He added no restrictions as to time, place, nationality, and the like, then they were laws, in the same sense as the natural laws established by God—those governing motion, gravity, sound and such. They simply work.

Sitting in a big stuffed chair morning after morning in my living room, poring over the Scriptures, praying, thinking, making notes on a yellow legal pad, I uncovered one, then two, and three, and more of these major principles. But, equally important, I put them to work in my life, my family's life, and the life of the Christian Broadcasting Network. I wasn't interested in abstraction. I wanted to determine if they worked.

They did. And they do. They, and they alone, can alter the world's slide into anarchy or dictatorship. They offer a third choice.

PART I
TWO DOMAINS

ONE

THE VISIBLE WORLD

The world is in crisis. That's the way *News-week* and *Time* magazines say it.

The ax is already laid at the root of the trees.[1] That's the way the Bible says it.

They're describing the same thing, merely from different viewpoints. The world has reached the stage where disaster looms on every hand. Everything seems to be going wrong, and the forecast is worse.

The key words in any description of our plight are economy, defense, energy, crime, poverty, morality, education, hunger, and pollution. Volumes are written on each. And each carries the same theme—hopelessness. The great cosmic clock appears to have wound down.

---

[1]Matthew 3:10.

All about us we see "fear in a handful of dust," in Eliot's words, as man stares horror-stricken at

> A heap of broken images, where the sun beats,
> And the dead tree gives no shelter, the cricket
> no relief,
> And the dry stone no sound of water.[2]

We cry out for solutions to problems too big for us. Our governments are on the verge of collapse; our finance is chaotic, our atmosphere polluted, our populations so massive that millions starve. Fear reigns.

Our condition is not difficult to understand. And the purpose of this book is not to dwell on that condition, but rather to explore reliable remedies. Nonetheless, to understand the encompassing nature of those remedies, we should take a few moments to set the stage of the visible world. We need only trace a few strands of the hangman's noose that seems poised over our heads, beginning with the most immediately destructive, the threat of nuclear holocaust.

Age of Terror

Let us go back to 1940. Three physicists—Enrico Fermi, Leo Szilard, and Eugene Wigner—working in a makeshift laboratory in a handball court under the grandstand at the University of Chicago, split the atom and thereby confirmed the theoretical formula of Albert Einstein: $E = MC^2$. The split, or fission, caused a multiplication of energy in the order of six million to one.

At last man had found a source of cheap and abundant energy for the world forever. A new industrial revolution was at hand.

---

[2]From "The Waste Land," T. S. Eliot, 1922.

Age-old territorial disputes would end. Wars would cease. The poor could be warmed, sheltered, fed. No nation need be without.

History records a different outcome. The work of those three deeply religious men evolved into an age of terror, not an age of abundance. There was Hiroshima. Then Nagasaki.

That was only the beginning. Physicists quickly perfected nuclear fusion and a release of energy of fifty million to one. Utilizing hydrogen, a fuel as abundant as the waters of the seas, this process held promise as the energy source of the millenium. There need be no fossil fuel shortage, no air pollution, no fabulously wealthy OPEC oil cartel, and no desperately poor Third World.

The utopia did not come. Instead we have hydrogen bombs rated in millions of tons of TNT. The superpower nations, during the fifties and sixties, built arsenals capable of destroying all life on earth. A balance of terror developed between the United States and the Soviet Union bearing the terrifying acronym MAD—Mutual Assured Destruction.

Then came the seventies. The United States, wearied by its struggle in Southeast Asia, gradually dismantled its military capability, delaying the start of weapons systems commensurate with advanced technology. The Soviet Union, meanwhile, pushed its flagging economy to the breaking point to build the most awesome array of weapons ever assembled by a nation in peacetime.

Instead of balance, the world of the eighties is faced with an imbalance of terror in favor of a malevolent dictatorship bent on world domination.

Aggravating the danger is the internal weakness of the Soviet Union. Its economy is falling apart. Its citizens see Marxism as a failure. Its leadership is old. In short, Communism does not appear to work.

A widely held view in the West is that these seemingly overwhelming difficulties might force the failing Soviet leaders to begin a military adventure simply to continue in power.

Given this view, plus the unquestioned Soviet military power, along with the vulnerability of the government's controlling Middle East oil, our age appears to have in place the ingredients to touch off World War III.

Age of terror is an apt description. But there is a solution, as we will see.

The Struggle for Energy

Intertwined with the age of terror is the concern for sufficient energy to fuel the gulping planet. It is almost as ominous as the nuclear threat, despite the deceptive ebb and flow in short-range supply and demand.

In 1950 there were 2.51 billion people in the world. By 1980 the figure had soared to 4.41 billion. The demand for everything from food to factories skyrocketed.

But nothing exploded like the demand for energy. In 1950 the world used the equivalent of 2.66 billion metric tons of coal. In 1980 consumption was *9.5 billion* metric tons.

In thirty years the population had not quite doubled; energy use had more than tripled. We were running wild with everything that required fuel.

This massive growth presented a simple truth as the decade of the eighties got underway: The planet does not contain enough nonrenewable and renewable sources of energy to supply the basic needs and growing aspirations of a population due to total nearly five billion by 1985.

It seems clear that if we do not make drastic cuts, we face the following perilous prospects:

—Those possessing dwindling energy sources will extract ever-increasing prices. If recent patterns continue, the cost will place such insupportable burdens on worldwide industry and financial markets that money supplies will be imprudently increased. This could set off hyperinflation and lead to worldwide financial collapse.

—To prolong high-energy lifestyles, the developed nations may use military force to seize dwindling resources. This could be expected to pit the United States against the Soviet Union ultimately, with all the risks of nuclear war or of surrender to intimidation.

—As oil import costs continue to mount, industrially developed nations will show more and more strain as they try to maintain a balance of trade. Aggressive financial actions, including punitive trade measures, seem certain and will heighten world tension.

—The prognosis is even worse for the weaker nations. They simply do not have the money to buy oil and pay interest on their huge debts at the same time. Many face bankruptcy already. Such default, by any of several nations could cause suffering internally and global economic confusion externally. It could trigger a worldwide bank collapse, for example, unless the United States is willing to bail out the country in trouble.

—America's cities pose a unique danger that has wide-ranging potential, traceable in large part to energy consumption and high costs. The mammoth office buildings, shopping centers, and apartment houses of New York, Detroit, Chicago, Cleveland, Boston, Philadelphia, and other cities are energy gluttons. The rising operating costs have been staggering. Compounding this financial burden is the fact that the physical plants of these cities—the sewers, water lines, and other underground support utilities, plus the roads, bridges, and other systems above ground—have far exceeded their life expectancies. The cities don't have the money for proper maintenance and replacement. Time bombs are ticking away both above and below ground. Should they begin to explode, the cities will be brought to their knees. The social and economic consequences nationally and globally will be staggering.

—Imprudent substitution of hazardous, untested energy sources in the face of diminishing traditional sources could present the world with intolerable environmental problems affecting all of life. Yet rigid regulation could inhibit exploration, discovery, and creativity needed to overcome shortages. The dilemma breeds deep strife.

—The reluctance and/or inability of car manufacturers to respond to worldwide energy problems has thrown a major portion of American industry into a tailspin that threatens the wider economy. By the early eighties, foreign car manufacturers, led by the Japanese, had seized 28 percent of U.S. domestic auto business. With one out of six people working in jobs related to the manufacturing of automobiles, profound changes are threatening 35 million Americans and their families. Anger and discontent are mounting.

The struggle for energy and the manifold ramifications of that struggle have propelled the world to the brink of upheaval. Even the tiniest of international movements has the potential for escalating.

We will see, however, that there are alternatives.

Economic Disaster

Picking up another related thread, we learn that the lesser-developed nations of the world owed more than $500 billion to banks and wealthier nations early in 1981. Annual interest on those loans approached $100 billion, which was $35 billion more than the total debt of those nations only eight years earlier. Tragically, they are being forced to borrow simply to pay interest. A number of loans are being refinanced so the nations do not appear to be in default.

During this period, Poland has been in the news as its people suffered the penalty of reaching for freedom from Soviet-led repression. That country's disastrous financial condition is typical of that of many other countries of the world. It owes $24 billion of the $89 billion owed to the West by Russia and the East Bloc countries. Strife-torn, it cannot pay its debts and yet has to ask for more.

It seems certain, with so many countries in a condition like Poland's, that one day a scene similar to the following will be played out:

A sweaty-palmed finance minister from Zaire or Turkey or East Germany will sit in a room in Switzerland or Germany or France and be told by several dignified bankers that his country's loans are in default. No more money is available. When word leaks out, the canny finance minister from oil-rich Kuwait, Abu Dhabi, Saudi Arabia, Iraq, or Libya could quietly withdraw his country's deposits from the banks in question. When word of this withdrawal is circulated, a wild scramble to get cash out of weakening banks could result.

Major institutions could fall like dominoes overnight. Eurodollar certificates of deposit could be wiped out, along with other large domestic certificates. Broad-based money market funds could lose virtually all their bank assets. There would very possibly have to be a nationwide freeze on bank withdrawals in this country to prevent a collapse of the banking system. Bonds, stocks, gold, silver, and jewels would fall like stones. Trade and commerce could be brought to a standstill.

Only a multinational effort to print a trillion or more dollars could stave off fiscal disaster. And this rescue would merely accelerate post-World War I, German-style hyperinflation, followed eventually by a worse crash.

In 1974–75 the world economy lurched, and several big banks and real estate operations failed; but the system held together. In 1980 it lurched again. That time silver crashed and the bond market lost $300 billion. Many financial institutions became technically insolvent as the market value of their bond and mortage portfolios plunged in the wake of a 21 percent prime interest rate. One major bank failed and Chrysler became a government ward, but the system survived.

Another lurch seems to be building. Banks have neither restored liquidity as they had after the mid-seventies problem nor have their portfolios improved as much as desired. Nonbank businesses are illiquid and overextended with short-term loans made in hopes that interest rates would drop.

Furthermore, the U. S. Government continues to borrow to cover budget deficits. Inflation, although dipping at least temporarily, still remains critical. It seems built into the system at every level. Prices do not actually fall; their rate of increase merely slows.

Questions are inevitable. Are major business and financial institutions, as well as individuals, bound for bankruptcy? Will this trigger the sort of doomsday scenario described above?

There are options, as we will see.

A Tailspin in Morality

As the eighties unfold, nothing portrays our world crisis more clearly than man's internal and moral condition. The unmistakable scent of what the Bible calls the antichrist spirit is in the air. It was present at the tower of Babel and at Sodom and Gomorrah. It was present in the French Revolution and in Nazi Germany. And it is present in Europe and the United States today.

The signs of this spirit are clear. They emerge in this fashion: A significant minority, then an actual majority, of the people in a society begin to throw off the restraints of history, then the restraints of written law, then accepted standards of morality, then established religion, and, finally, God Himself.

As the rebellion gains momentum, the participants grow bolder. Those practices that once were considered shameful and unlawful move into the open. Soon the practitioners are aggressive, militant. As each societal standard falls, another comes under attack. The pressure is relentless. Established institutions crumble. Ultimately the struggle that began as a cry for "freedom of expression" grows into all-out war against the rights of advocates of traditional morality. The latter are hated, reviled, isolated, and then persecuted.

Honor, decency, honesty, self-control, sexual restraint, family values, and sacrifice are replaced by gluttony, sensuality, bizarre sexual practices, cruelty, profligacy, dishonesty, delinquency, drunkenness, drug-induced euphoria, fraud, waste, debauched currency, and rampant inflation.

The people then search for a deity that will both permit and personify their basest desires. At Babel it was a tower, man's attempt to glorify himself. In ancient Mediterranean cultures, like those of Sodom and Gomorrah, it was a god or goddess of sex. In France, it was the goddess of reason; in Germany, Hitler and the Nazi party; in Europe and especially in the United States, the god of central government under the religion of secular humanism.

The pattern is always the same. So is the result. No society falling under the grip of the antichrist spirit has survived. First comes a period of lawlessness and virtual anarchy, then an economic collapse followed by a reign of terror. Then comes a strong dictator who plunders society for his personal aggrandizement; he dreams of worldwide empire and storms into war. Eventually come defeat and collapse.

In some cases God intervenes directly to destroy the antichrist society before it reaches full flower. In others, the society destroys itself. Sometimes a righteous nation takes action; in others the task is performed by stronger barbarians. But always there is destruction.

29

In the United States, trends, also reflected in other countries, are well defined:

—Organized crime is the largest industry in the land. With gross revenues of $150 billion, the profits of crime eclipse the profits of the American oil or auto industries, producing power and influence that compromise and corrupt the fabric of society. The impact of illegal drug use, as only one example, is staggering. In 1981 cocaine grossed $35 billion and marijuana $24 billion, establishing that Americans spent more on those two illegal drugs than they contributed to all charities, education, and religion combined.

—The sexual revolution has snaked its way into the schools, the homes, and virtually all of society. Traditional standards regarding nudity, fornication, adultery, homosexuality, incest, and sadomasochism have been under fierce attack and many are crumbling. Educators deluded by humanism are offering sex education without moral standards to children; some courses appear to advocate masturbation, premarital sex, and homosexuality. Motion pictures, television, and the publishing industry pour the excesses of unbridled gratification into communities and homes.

—From this rampant hedonism has emerged permission to minimize the inconvenient side effects of sexual pleasure. The Supreme Court ruled that the thing conceived through sexual relations between two humans is not itself a human and therefore may be destroyed prior to the fourth month of pregnancy. The killing of unborn infants through abortion has thus proceeded at the rate of 1.2 million a year.

—At the same time, family life has been battered. In the decade of the seventies, the number of couples living together outside of marriage doubled, and divorce reached a rate of one for every two marriages. But data were not crystallized for the marred lives of children caught in the break up of families, for the suicides of young and old unable to survive the trauma of sudden rootlessness, for the wasted lives of despair.

—Financial morality has been corrupted as the government, exalted by humanist philosophy, has become god and provider. In 1941 the population of the United States was 133.7 million; government spending was $13.6 billion. Forty years later the population had grown by 72 percent, to 229.3 million; federal spending had grown by 4,762 percent, to $661.2 billion. We have already touched on the result: federal debt exceeding $1 trillion, ever-increasing inflation, and domestic and world economies in danger of collapse.

—As self-restraint and regard for God rapidly diminish under the assault of secular humanism, a new rule of law has been emerging. Judges are less inclined to make decisions based on the Bible, the Constitution, natural law, or precedent. Instead, they often impose as a rule of law whatever seems sociologically expedient or whatever reflects the prevailing sentiment of the ruling elite. As Justice Charles Evans Hughes declared early in the century, "The Constitution is what the judges say it is," pointing to a trend in which a government based on men's opinons would supersede a government based on law. Lawlessness has thus come a long way.

But we will see that there is a remedy.

Revolt Against God

Underlying all the threads we have examined as integral to the deepening crisis coming upon the world—and we have examined only a fraction of them—is one that transcends all others. It is the increased disregard for the Creator of the world.

Shortly after the turn of the century, a false view of reality began to take hold in America. Although its name did not become well known immediately, humanism spread into all aspects of life and became the dominant philosophical view about the time of World War II. Today millions of people openly embrace it, and many millions more follow along under its influence.

Francis A. Schaeffer, the Christian philosopher-theologian, described humanism's influence this way:

> . . . the humanist world view includes many thousands of adherents and today controls the consensus in society, much of the media, much of what is taught in our schools, and much of the arbitrary law being produced by the various departments of government.
>
> The term humanism used in this wider, more prevalent way means Man beginning from himself, with no knowledge except what he himself can discover and no standards outside of himself. In this view Man is the measure of all things, as the Enlightenment expressed it.
>
> . . . Since [the humanists'] concept of Man is mistaken, their concept of society and of law is mistaken, and they have no sufficient base for either society or law.
>
> They have reduced Man to even less than his natural finiteness by seeing him only as a complex arrangement of molecules, made complex by blind chance. Instead of seeing him as something great who is significant even in his sinning, they see Man in his essence only as an intrinsically competitive animal, that has no other basic operating principle than natural selection brought about by the strongest, the fittest, ending on top. And they see Man as acting in this way both individually and collectively as society.[3]

Thus, for a vast number of people, God has been removed from the center of things, and man has taken His place. All things exist for man and his pleasure.

In a church-state dialogue sponsored in 1981 by the Virginia Council of Churches, a professor of humanistic studies summed

---

[3]Francis A. Schaeffer, *A Christian Manifesto* (Chicago: Crossway, 1981), pp. 24,26.

up the direction of American leadership most clearly: "We must throw off the tyranny of the concept that the Bible is the Word of God. We must be freed from the tyranny of thought that comes from Martin Luther, John Calvin, Zwingli, and John Knox."

He discarded the Bible as the authoritative guide for faith and conduct, casting with it such long-accepted truths as the doctrine of man's sinfulness, the doctrine of eternal reward and eternal punishment, the necessity for repentance and justification by faith in Jesus Christ, and the necessity for holy living to please God. Such astounding recommendations can only be grasped when one recalls the words of *Humanist Manifesto I* and *II* (produced in 1933 and 1973), which denied the "existence of a supernatural God who hears and answers prayer."

With all standards and yardsticks removed, society first eased, then rushed toward the extremes of hedonism and nihilism, with increasing numbers finding fulfillment in "doing their own thing."

"If it feels good, do it," comes the advice of everyone from parents to psychologists. This, they say, is freedom.

Meanwhile, as we noted earlier, nothing works. Bodies wear out early as sickness and disease soar. Never has there been so much cancer, so much heart disease. Brains, too, wear out. Never have emotional and mental breakdowns run so high; never have suicides reached such levels. Schools fail; businesses fail; governments fail.

Yes, humanism and its society are failing, although seemingly few have perceived the depth of that failure. Most see only symptoms, not the underlying sickness.

Inevitable Conclusions

The fear has become widespread that our society—and the world's—is beyond repair. There is confusion everywhere.

33

At times the confusion approaches chaos. It seems clear that we will slide further into chaos, the jungle of anarchy—"I've got mine; to heck with you"—"do unto others before they can do unto you"—"every man for himself." Or we in desperation will yield to dictatorship. Which will it be?

It matters not that both of the prevailing philosophies of materialism have been proven corrupt and ineffective. Communism says materialism is the goal but that the state should control it. Capitalism strives for materialism, but the strong control it. Both move toward dictatorship, oligarchical or individual.

Eventually a strong man must be chosen as both systems fail—unless we turn to the third choice that is available to us.

What will we do?

TWO

THE INVISIBLE WORLD

🍃 Fortunately, a Voice speaks steadily and clearly into the turmoil and dread of the day, a Voice that contradicts our finitude and limitation and restriction. It says, " 'But seek first His kingdom and His righteousness; and all these things shall be added to you.' "[1]

Obviously the words are those of Jesus, climaxing a teaching about food, clothing, shelter, and all the "things" needed for life. God, His heavenly Father, was able and eager to provide the necessities for happy, successful living on the planet Earth if the people merely turned to the right place—His kingdom.

His point immediately established a fact that the world has in large measure refused to consider—the fact that an invisible world undergirds, surrounds, and interpenetrates the visible

---

[1]Matthew 6:33.

world in which we live. Indeed, it controls the visible world, for it is unrestricted, unlimited, infinite.

The problem of the world, and of many Christians, has not been simply refusing to acknowledge the possibility of such a kingdom, but failing to perceive that it exists *right now*, not in some far-off time or far-off place called heaven. This is so strange because Jesus spent virtually all of His earthly ministry telling people that the kingdom of God had come and then explaining its workings.

For reasons that are beyond our comprehension, even we Christians missed it as we soaked up the good news of salvation, the fullness of the Holy Spirit, the fellowship of the church, and the *future* millenium. In fact, it is embarrassing today, as we begin to glimpse the core of what Jesus was doing, to note that practically everything He said pertained to the "kingdom." For example, His first utterance in His public ministry, according to Matthew, was: " 'Repent, for the kingdom of heaven is at hand.' "[2]

Each of the gospel writers said it similarly. "The time has come," Jesus declared, in essence. "The kingdom is here, and I've come to open it to you and to show you how it works."

His pattern recalls the days following the anointing of Saul as Israel's first king when it became necessary for the prophet Samuel to teach how things should work: "Then Samuel told the people the manner of the kingdom, and wrote it in a book, and laid it up before the LORD. . . ."[3] Jesus did much the same, teaching His followers "the manner of the kingdom," but leaving it to others to put it in writing.

Many of us are now discovering this central purpose of our Lord, perceiving that the kingdom of God, though invisible, is right now nonetheless real, nonetheless powerful. We are much

---

[2]Matthew 4:17.
[3]1 Samuel 10:25, KJV.

like the servant of Elisha who went outside the tent one morning and saw Syrian troops ready to close in on them from every side. "We're surrounded!" he yelled.

But Elisha calmly asked the Lord to open the young man's eyes. Then he saw into the invisible world. Chariots of fire, the heavenly host, were everywhere about them, protecting Elisha. As the prophet had said, " '. . . those who are with us are more than those who are with them.' "[4]

Yes, the kingdom of God is here—now. And the message of the Bible is that we can and should look from this visible world, which is finite, into the invisible world, which is infinite. We should look from a world filled with impossibilities into one filled with possibilities.

We should do more than look, however, if we believe the Scriptures. We should enter. We should reach from the visible into the invisible and bring that secret kingdom into the visible through its principles—principles that can be adopted at this moment.

"The kingdom of God is like this . . . ," Jesus said, in effect. "It operates this way. . . ." "If you want this, then do this. . . ." Over and over.

So real is this invisible world, that when Jesus comes to earth the second time things will be turned inside out—through a sort of skinning process, you might say—and the invisible will become visible. The kingdom of God and its subjects will be manifested—unveiled. In the language of Paul's letter to the Romans: ". . . the creation waits eagerly for the revealing of the sons of God."[5] It "groans and suffers"—"standing on tiptoe," according to J. B. Phillips' translation—as it yearns for that unveiling.

The apostles had a foretaste of the inside-out effect during

---

[4]2 Kings 6:16.
[5]Romans 8:19.

their days with Jesus. First came a statement by the Lord that has puzzled many Bible readers through the centuries: " 'Truly I say to you, there are some of those who are standing here who shall not taste death until they see the Son of Man coming in His kingdom.' "[6]

A most marvelous event occurred six days later. We refer to it as the Transfiguration. Taking Peter, James, and John with Him, Jesus went to a high mountain.

And He was transfigured before them; and His face shone like the sun, and His garments became as white as light. And behold, Moses and Elijah appeared to them, talking with Him. And Peter answered and said to Jesus, "Lord, it is good for us to be here; if You wish, I will make three tabernacles here, one for You, and one for Moses, and one for Elijah." While he was still speaking, behold, a bright cloud overshadowed them; and behold, a voice out of the cloud, saying, "This is My beloved Son, with whom I am well-pleased; listen to Him!" And when the disciples heard this, they fell on their faces and were much afraid. And lifting up their eyes, they saw no one, except Jesus Himself alone.[7]

The Lord became like lightning, shining white, and what had been invisible within Him became visible. The inside became the outside. The Law (Moses) and the prophets (Elijah) were fulfilled, and the Son of Man (Jesus) came visibly in His kingdom, in power and glory.

The disciples had a taste of what the kingdom will be at its manifestation. But what they saw at that moment had been resident in Jesus all the time. It had merely been invisible, but no less real and powerful. And that is what the Lord was telling His followers to lay hold of when He instructed them to seek the kingdom *first* so all of their needs would be met.

---

[6]Matthew 16:28.
[7]Matthew 17:2–6,8.

"Reach into the invisible and apply it to the visible," He said. " 'For all things are possible with God.' "[8]

The Unlimited World of Jesus

Almighty God has been warning for thousands of years that because of our foolishness we will face crises. We are face to face with nuclear terror, a massive energy shortage, an insoluble economic crisis, debilitating moral bankruptcy, and other impossible difficulties. But Jesus explained that we are limited in our ability to cope with such problems only because we insist on living according to the ways of a world that is limited.

In effect he has said, "That need not remain so. An unlimited world surrounds you.

"You are finite; it is infinite.

"You are mortal; it is immortal.

"You are filled with impossibilities; it is filled with possibilities."

That was the world of Jesus, even when He came as a man to live on this finite earth. He was careful to say: " '. . . the Son can do nothing of Himself, unless it is something He sees the Father doing; for whatever the Father does, these things the Son also does in like manner.' "[9]

The invisible world of His Father was Jesus' world throughout His incarnation. It was a world where everything was beautiful. And He became upset when His disciples failed to follow His example.

Once, when they were in the middle of the Sea of Galilee on a boat journey Jesus had instructed them to make, a storm arose;

---

[8]Mark 10:27.
[9]John 5:19.

and their mission was near failure as their little vessel was swamped and showed signs of sinking. They rushed to wake Him from a much-needed nap. He was visibly perplexed. Why hadn't they been able to cope with the situation? They had failed to see into the invisible world where there were no impediments to the Lord's mission, and they had allowed themselves to be limited by world conditions.

So Jesus Himself arose and spoke to the storm, calming it. He then asked a rather humbling question: " 'Why are you timid, you men of little faith' "[10]

They had refused to reach into the world of the possible. And Jesus was angry, frustrated by the unwillingness of those He loved to accept the truth of what He had told them. One cannot help but wonder about His frustration as His followers seem so impotent to overcome the visible world today.

A Major Lesson

The Gospel according to Mark contains one of the Lord's most compact, yet most comprehensive, teachings about how to manifest the power of the invisible world in the visible today. Although we will be exploring the passage in more detail later, it is so significant for our initial understanding of the kingdom that we need to look at it in part now.

Jesus set the stage for the teaching when, on the way with His disciples to the temple to deal with the mockery practiced there under the guise of worship, He walked up to a fig tree in leaf, examined it for fruit, found none, and said: " 'May no one ever eat fruit from you again!' "[11]

We must understand immediately that Jesus was not being

---

[10]Matthew 8:26.
[11]Mark 11:14.

capricious or petulant. He didn't simply lose His temper. The fig tree, as is so often the case in Scripture, symbolized Israel in biblical times; and when He cursed it, He was symbolically addressing a religious system that was often outwardly showy and inwardly fruitless. It was a system that practiced money changing and the selling of doves for sacrifice within the temple walls but gave the people little to feed their souls. He cursed that practice, too, as the Scripture goes on to report, and drove the money changers from the premises: " 'Is it not written, "My house shall be called a house of prayer for all the nations"? But you have made it a robbers' den.' "[12]

No, He was not showing off. As with everything in His brief time on earth, the Lord made a point of tremendous significance. The next morning it came to light.

Jesus and His disciples passed the fig tree on the way back into Jerusalem and it had died, withered under His curse. Still failing to perceive the invisible world but yet observing its effects, Peter blurted out, "Look, the fig tree you cursed is all dried up!"

Then came the simplest insight into the deepest phenomenon: "And Jesus answered saying to them, 'Have faith in God.' "[13]

Those four words burst through the frontiers of heaven, laying bare the invisible kingdom. *Have faith in God.* We must totally believe in and trust Almighty God. We must know that One sits on the throne of the universe, as John saw in his great vision in the Book of the Revelation;[14] and He controls everything to the uttermost. He is without peer. He is omnipotent, omniscient, and omnipresent—the only free, unrestricted being in the universe.

Kathryn Kuhlman often said during her powerful ministry, "I sometimes think we're too familiar with God." She was right.

---

[12]Mark 11:17.
[13]Mark 11:22.
[14]See Revelation 4:2.

Many times it seems we are trying to make Him into a toy that we can wind up and get to do our bidding. We sing Him little songs and utter all manner of things that threaten to demean His utter sovereignty. Kathryn's point was that God is God Almighty, the Great I Am. He created the sun and the moon and the earth and the solar system. It is staggering! He merely said, "Let there be light"[15] and the power of a billion hydrogen bombs began to move, rolling from one end of the solar system to the other. The distances and the energy are awesome. And they clearly illustrate the truth that a power exists in the universe transcending anything finite man's tiny mind can imagine. Paul the apostle put it into words, but even they are inadequate: "Now to Him who is able to do exceeding abundantly beyond all that we ask or think. . . ."[16]

That is God. And Jesus said, "Have faith in Him." Touch Him, He said, and anything is possible.

The Lord wants us in league with His Father. His teachings make it plain that total faith and trust in God—for every breath and every second—are to produce a oneness with Him. We are to see with Him, think with Him, as Jesus did, so that we can say along with Jesus that we do only what we see the Father doing. That way, we will reach into the invisible world even though living in the visible.

In the fig tree episode, Jesus went on to explain another point that will be dealt with fully in another chapter, but for now we will simply reflect on it:

"Truly I say to you, whoever says to this mountain, 'Be taken up and cast into the sea,' and does not doubt in his heart, but believes that what he says is going to happen, it shall be *granted* him. Therefore I say to you, all things for which you pray and ask, believe that you have received them, and they shall be *granted* you."[17]

---

[15]Genesis 1:14.
[16]Ephesians 3:20.
[17]Mark 11:23,24.

In short, Jesus told His disciples that if they truly had faith in God, believed in His absolute sovereignty and mighty power, and entered into league with Him, they would become participants in the same energy and power that prevailed at the creation. They would work as God works; be fellow workers with Him, in the words of Paul.[18]

Yes, Jesus said, there is an invisible world, but we can see into it and touch it—here, now. God works; He wants us to work.

Principles of the Kingdom

Having been trained and surrounded by Christians who did not concern themselves especially with the Lord's teachings on the reality of the kingdom here and now, I didn't begin to catch glimpses of this reality in any meaningful way until the mid-seventies. I, too, had dwelt pretty much on the good news of salvation and the work of the Holy Spirit in believers' lives, and that truly is good news. But there is much more.

By mid-decade, I was wrestling with John the Baptist's insistence that "the kingdom of heaven is at hand."[19] As I have said, I soon saw he was reporting that the kingdom was here—here on earth—obviously because Jesus Christ was here.

I mused over this for many weeks and months, tracking through the Scriptures, praying for wisdom, and talking with one or two friends. As I badgered the Lord for wisdom, I began to realize there are principles in the kingdom as enunciated by Jesus Christ and that they are as valid for our lives as the laws of thermodynamics or the law of gravity. The physical laws are immutable, and I soon saw that the kingdom laws are equally so.

How can we determine those principles? They are found in the Bible. When we see a statement of Jesus that is not qualified as to

---

[18]1 Corinthians 3:9.
[19]Matthew 3:2.

43

time or recipient, then we have uncovered a universal truth. If He uses the terms "whosoever" or "whatsoever" or some other sweeping generalization, we should be especially alert. He is probably declaring a truth that will apply in every situation, in every part of the world, in every time.

It sounds so simple, and it is. Not every word spoken by the Lord had direct application for everyone; some were restricted. But others were without restriction—a "house divided against itself shall not stand,"[20] for example.

Once we perceive this secret, we realize anew that the Bible is not an impractical book of theology, but rather a practical book of life containing a system of thought and conduct that will guarantee success. And it will be true success, true happiness, true prosperity, not the fleeting, flashy, inconsistent success the world usually settles for.

The Bible, quite bluntly, is a workable guidebook for politics, government, business, families, and all the affairs of mankind.

There are dozens of these principles sprinkled throughout, and they are all marvelous. But there are several broad, overriding ones that I like to think of as "laws" of the kingdom. They span all of life, often overlapping and supplementing one another, but never contradicting. We will be probing into those major ones that hold special potential for revolutionizing our time and world.

They give us an alternative in our current world dilemma.

Now Is the Time

Think for a moment about those strange words of Jesus: " '. . . seek first His kingdom and His righteousness; and all these things shall be added to you.' "[21]

---

[20]Matthew 12:25.
[21]Matthew 6:33.

So many of us see the words and are conscience-stricken. But for the wrong reasons.

We say, "Oh, if I could only bring myself to pray a lot and read the Bible and go to church every day, then God would like me and I would be His, and He would send His blessing to me."

We are not even certain we understand what we mean when we say "blessing."

Jesus was much more concrete than that. He was saying, "The kingdom of God rules in the affairs of men. It has principles for living, and they will bring success." Indeed, they will bring forth the kinds of things the world needs so desperately—the food, the shelter, the clothing, the fuel, the happiness, the health, the peace.

"But you shouldn't spend all your time and concentration seeking those things," He said in effect. "Seek the kingdom, understand the way it works, and then, as day follows night and as spring follows winter, the evidences of earthly success will follow you."

If we press this through to its logical conclusion, possibilities for life will rise up that we long ago relegated to the musty, unused portions of our Bibles, thinking of them as those promises made for a future time referred to as "the millenium." We will see that many of those conditions—those blessings we feared might turn out to be lofty Bible language that would pass us by—can be experienced in large measure right now. For they exist in the kingdom now. And we are speaking of reaching into that kingdom and letting its principles govern us right now.

Only God will inaugurate the visible reign on earth of His Son and those who will rule with Him,[22] but His word for the last two thousand years has been to "prepare the way."[23] His purpose is that His people know Him and learn how His secret kingdom functions. For the most part, we have fallen far short. But the

---

[22]See Revelation 20:4.
[23]Matthew 3:3.

word persists, and we can readily expect the willing fulfillment of some of the millenium blessings, like those foreseen by the prophet Isaiah, if we will follow His instructions:

They will not hurt or destroy in all My holy mountain,
For the earth will be full of the knowledge of the LORD
As the waters cover the sea.[24]

. . . they will hammer their swords into plowshares, and their spears into pruning hooks.
Nation will not lift up sword against nation,
And never again will they learn war.[25]

There *can* be peace; there *can* be plenty; there *can* be freedom. They will come the minute human beings accept the principles of the invisible world and begin to live by them in the visible world.

Can mankind do that? We will see how.

---

[24]See Isaiah 11:9.
[25]Isaiah 2:4.

THREE
SEEING AND ENTERING

$\mathbf{\mathit{k}S^{\wedge}_{\bigcirc}}$ In New Testament times, there was a man who
perceived there was more to Jesus than met the eye. He may have
heard John the Baptist refer to Him as one who " 'existed before
me.'"[1] The strange prophet, who lived alone in the desert, had
even called Him " 'the son of God.'"[2] Jesus of Nazareth was real
and down-to-earth. Yet there was something other-worldly about
Him. He spoke with authority, like the authority of Jehovah
written about in the scrolls.[3] He must have been sent from
heaven.[4]

One night this man, Nicodemus,[5] a ruler of the Jews, found
Jesus alone and managed to talk with Him, which was hard to do

---

[1]John 1:30.
[2]John 1:34.
[3]See Matthew 7:29.
[4]See Matthew 16:16.
[5]See John 3:1–21.

because of the crowds. He may have been glad no one would see him.

He fumbled a bit for something to say and then blurted out: "Rabbi, we know you've come from God as a teacher, for no one can do the signs You do unless God is with him."

It was an awkward start, but it summarized what he was feeling. Nicodemus wanted to know God, and he instinctively realized that Jesus could give him teaching that would lead directly to God.

The Lord skipped small talk and went to the heart of Nicodemus' concern, preserving for all generations an understanding of the indispensable initial step toward life in an invisible world that governs all else. The kingdom of God is not really a place—at least not yet—but rather a state of being in which men, women, and children have yielded all sovereignty to the one and only true sovereign, Almighty God. It is the rule of God in the hearts, minds, and wills of people—the state in which the unlimited power and blessing of the unlimited Lord are forthcoming.

The natural eye cannot see this domain, and Jesus quickly explained that. He probably spoke softly, but distinctly. " '. . . unless one is born again, he cannot *see* the kingdom of God.' "[6]

Nicodemus was startled. What kind of a remark was that? So, getting bolder, he answered back more directly than he had begun: " 'How can a man be born when he is old? He cannot enter a second time into his mother's womb and be born, can he?' "[7]

The poor man had wanted to glimpse the invisible world and had been told how, but it went right by him, as it probably would have most of us. But Jesus really had told him how to peer into the throne room of God, from which the universe is directed. It

[6]John 3:3.
[7]John 3:4.

should be noted, however, that He referred first to "seeing" the kingdom. Next, He took it a step further: " ' . . . unless one is born of water and the Spirit, he cannot *enter* the kingdom of God.' "[8]

Jesus knew His man. Nicodemus wanted it all. He had suspected this very special rabbi, although visibly a flesh-and-blood man, was somehow living at that moment in contact with God. So Jesus laid it out for him.

God is spirit. Those who would know Him—who would worship Him—must do so in spirit.[9] Since the Fall left man spiritually dead,[10] we must be reborn. Flesh begets flesh and spirit begets spirit,[11] so this rebirth must be accomplished by God the Holy Spirit. After that, being children of God,[12] we are able to engage in communion and fellowship with Him, as Adam did in the original kingdom in the Garden of Eden.[13]

Nicodemus' amazement soared, so Jesus pressed on with many deep things of the spirit—the things that men and women everywhere must make a part of themselves if they are to begin to deal successfully with our world in crisis:

"Do not marvel that I said to you, 'You must be born again.' The wind blows where it wishes and you hear the sound of it, but do not know where it comes from and where it is going; so is everyone who is born of the Spirit." Nicodemus answered and said to Him, "How can these things be?" Jesus answered and said to him, "Are you the teacher of Israel, and do not understand these things? Truly, truly, I say to you, we speak that which we know, and bear witness of that which we have seen; and you do not receive our witness. If I told you earthly things and you do not believe, how shall you believe if I

---

[8]John 3:5.
[9]See John 4:24.
[10]See Genesis 2:17.
[11]See John 3:6.
[12]See John 1:12,13.
[13]See Genesis 1,2.

49

tell you heavenly things? And no one has ascended into heaven, but He who descended from heaven, even the son of Man. And as Moses lifted up the serpent in the wilderness, even so must the Son of Man be lifted up; that whoever believes may in Him have eternal life. For God so loved the world, that He gave His only begotten Son, that whoever believes in Him should not perish, but have eternal life."[14]

The New Testament evidence is that Nicodemus did eventually believe,[15] accepting entry into the secret kingdom even while coping with the trials of the visible one.

Like millions and millions of others, this once-timid man received Jesus into his life, accepting Him for who He was—God incarnate, the Word become flesh, Savior of the world, Lord of all. Forgiven for his sins, he was reconciled to God Almighty and enabled to perceive the "heavenly things" Jesus had spoken of, to gain access to the kingdom of God.

He was, in short, born again—born from above, as some translators prefer, born of the Spirit. He could say with Paul the apostle who later wrote:

Now we have received, not the spirit of the world, but the Spirit who is from God, that we might *know the things freely given to us by God,* which things we also speak, not in words taught by human wisdom, but in those taught by the Spirit, combining spiritual thoughts with spiritual words.[16]

Both Nicodemus and Paul discovered that the kingdom of heaven is based on an invisible, spiritual reality, capable of visible, physical effects.

This is the reality that the world craves so badly.

---

[14]John 3:8–16.
[15]John 19:38–42.
[16]1 Corinthians 2:12,13.

50

Rebirth Is a Beginning

Unhappily, evangelical Christians have for too long reduced the born-again experience to the issue of being "saved." Salvation is an important issue, obviously, and must never be de-emphasized. But rebirth must be seen as a beginning, not an arrival. It provides access to the invisible world, the kingdom of God, of which we are to learn and experience and then share with others. Jesus Himself said it clearly before His ascension:

"All authority has been given to Me in heaven and on earth. Go therefore and *make disciples* of all the nations, baptizing them in the name of the Father and the Son and the Holy Spirit, *teaching them to observe all that I commanded you;* and lo, I am with you always, even to the end of the age."[17]

The commission was to make followers and learners—converts—and to *teach* them the principles of the kingdom. Entry into the body of believers was not enough. They were to learn how to live in this world, although their residence was in the kingdom. The invisible was to rule the visible. Christ has authority over both.

We have fallen short. Occasionally we have perceived God's hand at work in the world. But we have not striven to understand how the kingdom functions nor have we fully participated in its manifestation on earth.

We *must* hear this before it is too late: Jesus has opened to us the truths of the secret world of God! He has given us entrance into a world of indescribable power.

The atom gives us a clue as to what we're dealing with. We can't see an atom; solid matter looks like solid matter. But atomic theory convinces us the atoms are there, pressed together into material substance at some point in time. And with Einstein's

---

[17]Matthew 28:18–20.

$E = MC^2$, we have discovered that this means matter is energy—sheer power capable of blowing up the world. Yet all we see is the matter, even though the energy controls the matter.

Now this terribly great power is a tiny fraction of what we touch when we touch God's power. And it, too, is unseen—totally undiscerned—by one who has not been born again. The unspiritual man or woman regards such possibilities as foolishness.[18] And even many who have been born anew by the Spirit, though possessing the internal eyesight to see and believe in the invisible realm, refrain from appropriating its power for their daily lives. Having "seen" the kingdom, but not having fully "entered" in, they allow the conditions of the world to dominate them, contrary to the instructions of the Lord. The rebirth should give us the power to prevail over circumstances surrounding us.

Jesus gave us an additional piece of insight on this score. If we are to enter into the kingdom, taking full hold of that which is available, then we must " 'become like children,' " He said.[19] That is hard for our sophisticated generation, for it requires simple trust. A child is willing to leap ahead and seize any opportunity his father lays before him. So it must be with Christians and their heavenly Father, who gladly offers them the inexhaustible riches and power of His kingdom.[20] Indeed, He is pressing them upon us, if we will only respond confidently, joyfully, exuberantly—like little children.

An Issue of Truth

In light of the critical condition of the world, we need to examine even more philosophically why we are falling short in

---

[18]See 1 Corinthians 2:14.
[19]Matthew 18:3.
[20]Luke 12:32.

the matter of entering into the kingdom after rebirth. For if Christians miss the mark, how will the *world* learn?

Let's look at the logic of the problem. It leads us right into the issue of truth; and if there is anything the people of the world are looking for, it's truth.

First, we should recall the teachings of the Lord delivered through His encounter with a woman of Samaria. It is remarkable that this discourse, containing spiritual instruction with practical physical effects, involved one from the despised Samaritans, a people of mixed Assyrian and Jewish blood resulting from the Assyrian invasion of the Israelites' land centuries earlier. The Lord, a Jew, obviously wanted to show that His message extended to all people. We pick up the conversation in the middle of profound insights into the Holy Spirit, eternal life, adultery, worship, and ministry to the world, with Jesus speaking:

". . . an hour is coming, and now is, when the true worshipers shall worship the Father in spirit and *truth;* for such people the Father seeks to be His worshipers. God is spirit, and those who worship Him must worship in spirit and *truth.*"[21]

That alone sounds right and good, but how does one practically do it?

Fortunately Jesus also said the following in a discussion with His disciples: " 'I am the way, and the *truth,* and the life. . . .' "[22]

Putting those two revelations together, we see that we are to bring ourselves into line with a standard that is true. Jesus is the *truth,* so, being born of His Spirit, we are to conform to Him. We are to walk in His will. Only then can we worship God in spirit and truth. Only then can we move in truth. Note how essential He said this was: " 'Not everyone who says to Me, "Lord,

---

[21]John 4:23,24.
[22]John 14:6.

Lord," will enter the kingdom of heaven; but *he who does the will of My Father* who is in heaven.' "[23]

We need to be clear on this. Truth is the very centerpiece of the kingdom and its principles. We must be certain of the essential rightness of the principles, as opposed to other views. They lead to a new system of life that is better than any other system, the most practical possible, providing peace of mind, health, happiness, abundance, joy, and life everlasting. But we believe them because they are *true*.

Consider the following dialogue between Jesus and Pontius Pilate, the Roman governor at the time of the Lord's arrest and crucifixion:

Then Pilate went back into the palace and called for Jesus to be brought to him. "Are you the King of the Jews?" he asked him. " 'King' as *you* use the word or as the *Jews* use it?" Jesus asked. "Am I a Jew?" Pilate retorted. "Your own people and their chief priests brought you here. Why? What have you done?" Then Jesus answered, "I am not an earthly king. If I were, my followers would have fought when I was arrested by the Jewish leaders. But my kingdom is not of the world." Pilate replied, "But you are a king then?" "Yes," Jesus said. "I was born for that purpose. *And I came to bring truth to the world. All who love the truth are my followers.*"[24]

Yes, there is a kingdom. Jesus said it is founded on truth. He, the Truth, is king of it. Everyone who loves the truth—Him—and wants to follow the truth is a member of that kingdom.

". . . He who sent Me is true; and the things which I heard from Him, these I speak to the world. . . . If you abide in My word, then you are truly disciples of Mine; and you shall know *the truth*, and *the truth shall make you free.*"[25]

---

[23]Matthew 7:21.
[24]John 18:33–37, TLB.
[25]John 8:26,31,32.

Not only is He true, the Lord said, but the things He teaches are true. And if we accept and practice these truths, we will be free, another condition the people of the world so desperately seek. I want to emphasize what it is that makes us free. It is not merely the acceptance of Jesus and His atonement, but *the doing of the truth* —putting into practice the principles of the kingdom.

As I said, we too often stop short. We must start with the crucifixion and the resurrection, but we must follow through with the practice of the principles, the laws of life. For God said thousands of years ago:

". . . I will give you a new heart and put a new spirit within you; and I will remove the heart of stone from your flesh and give you a heart of flesh. And I will put My spirit within you *and cause you to walk in My statutes, and you will be careful to observe my ordinances.*"[26]

He has gone to great lengths over many centuries to plant within our hearts His ways, His truth, His principles. What he has done surpasses the old covenant of law and regulation handed down to the people of Israel at Mount Sinai. Jesus has fulfilled the written law, placing it within His subjects, but they must live out the principles.

Applying this to our personal conduct, we see that speaking the truth is central. Its importance must never be minimized. Just as Jesus is the king of truth, the Holy Spirit (the Lord and giver of life) is called "the Spirit of truth."[27] Where He abides there is truth. At the same time, Satan (the adversary) is described as "the father of lies."[28]

Although true speech is only a part of ultimate truth, it is no

---

[26]Ezekiel 36:26,27.
[27]John 14:17.
[28]John 8:44.

mere coincidence that the apostle John tells us God's final heaven will exclude anyone who "maketh a lie."[29] All liars, he declares, "shall have their part in the lake which burneth with fire and brimstone."[30] Telling the truth is a serious matter!

In the world we see conduct that flies flagrantly in the face of these warnings. The Soviet Union, an atheistic society, gives over an entire section of its secret police to "disinformation"—the systematic spreading of lies through the free press of its adversaries. So frequent has the use of the big lie become in dictatorial societies that George Orwell in his book *1984* portrayed the ultimate dictatorship as one in which there was no truth, only a reordering of facts in "newspeak."

In the United States, regard for truth still exists in some quarters, although it is clearly diminishing along with regard for absolute values. Perjury—the willful telling of a lie while under lawful oath—is a felony and stands as a secular affirmation of the kingdom's demand for truth.

How sad that in some instances we find church people who actually seek to further God's kingdom by the use of falsehood, building up with one hand but tearing down with the other. Exaggeration, embellishment, and even fabrication have become instruments of evangelism in some quarters. A tragic indictment is that the term "evangelistically speaking" is the euphemism some have chosen to describe flagrant misrepresentation of fact.

We must see that the Lord does not need our embellishment to accomplish His purpose or to glorify His name. We do Him— and ourselves—a disservice when we depart from the truth.

Jesus Understands

Jesus and His Ways are true. As the One by whom and for whom all things were created,[31] He understands precisely how

---

[29]Revelation 21:27, KJV.
[30]Revelation 21:8, KJV.
[31]See Colossians 1:16.

the world works. His teachings, which so many in the world have tried to relegate to the categories of goody-goody daydreaming or pietistic navel-gazing, are functional.

The world yearns for peace; He can provide it. The world wants love; He has the formula. The world wants riches, honor, and full life; He promises them all.

But there are requisites. One must be born again by accepting the free gift of salvation that He alone provides, learn from Him, and put His principles into practice.

What are the key laws or principles that govern the deepest desires and needs of mankind? They embody the truths that we will be examining and illustrating in detail in the following chapters, along with the virtues and subprinciples flowing through them.

We will see that the truths of Jesus have the characteristic of the "truths" of the American Declaration of Independence—they are "self-evident." We will begin to understand why a society that abandons these laws, which are self-evident, will collapse. And equally evident will be the reasons why a society that voluntarily adheres to such laws can be expected to prosper.

Do not forget: The One proclaiming the laws knows how both the visible world and the invisible kingdom work!

FOUR

HOW GOD'S KINGDOM WORKS

To understand how the kingdom of heaven works and how it holds sway over the visible world, we must place two facts in the brightest light.

First, there is absolute abundance in the kingdom of God.

Second, it is possible to have total favor with the ruler of that abundance.

On the first point, Jesus, telling His disciples that they were being permitted to know the secrets of the kingdom,[1] set forth the truth of abundance with a parable about a sower.[2] The seed that fell on good ground, He said, yielded crops of a hundredfold, sixtyfold, and thirtyfold. *That* is abundance—returns of 10,000, 6,000, and 3,000 percent. You see, there is no economic recession, no shortage, in the kingdom of God.

---

[1]See Matthew 13:11.
[2]See Matthew 13:3–8.

Throughout our forests, we see this truth touching the physical world. Consider the profusion of seed that comes from a maple tree. Look at the multiplicity of colors in a sunset; there are more hues than we can name. Plant life, marine life, bird life—there is no end, almost as though God had sent abundance into the universe as testimony to His own infinitude.

Because He is the only truly free being in the universe, His kingdom is a sphere of total possibility. Jesus emphasized this when He multiplied the loaves and fish, taking a little boy's lunch and feeding more than five thousand hungry people.[3] God is never diminished by circumstances.

Neither is He limited by His own universe or the natural laws He Himself established. Pantheists attempt to convince us that God is merely *in* nature. But were that true, He would be limited. No, He is above the laws of nature and any restrictions that those laws might try to impose. He can create from nothing, or He can take existing matter and transform it. His is a total world—total health, total life, total energy, total strength, total provision.

In the matter of favor, Jesus, of course, was our perfect illustration of God's bestowal: "And Jesus kept increasing in wisdom and stature, and in *favor* with God and men."[4]

Within a few short years, God presented the supreme token of this grace at the time of the baptism of Jesus in the River Jordan: ". . . and the Holy Spirit descended upon Him in bodily form like a dove, and a voice came out of heaven, 'Thou art My beloved son, in Thee I am well-pleased.' "[5]

This, God the Father was saying, was the One He had spoken of and promised for centuries. He was going to pour out His grace and blessing on His only begotten Son and on those who belong to Him.

---

[3]See Matthew 14:16–21.
[4]Luke 2:52.
[5]Luke 3:22.

First, we need to recognize that when the Bible speaks of God's "grace," it is speaking of His "favor." In the New Testament, the Greek word for grace is *charis*, perhaps best defined as "the unmerited favor of God."

This favor, the apostle Paul said, allows us to stand before God Himself.[6] It is our sole means of access to the throne of the kingdom.[7] Think of it: If we have access to the Father, standing before Him in His favor, then we have the prospect of continuous blessing. Indeed, Paul wrote that the prospect was for *increasing* blessing:

But God, being rich in mercy, because of His great love with which He loved us, even when we were dead in our transgressions, made us alive together with Christ (by grace you have been saved), and raised us up with Him, and seated us with Him in the heavenly places, in Christ Jesus, in order that *in the ages to come He might show the surpassing riches of His grace* in kindness toward us in Christ Jesus.[8]

Now when God blesses us and keeps us, and lets His face shine upon us, and is gracious to us,[9] then before men we appear in a light that far transcends any of our natural abilities. He can cause our plans to succeed. He can cause people to like us. He can cause us to be preferred and chosen above others of equal talent. He can protect our children. He can guard our property. He can cause His angels to aid us.

How well I remember the day in the late sixties when God showed forth this favor in my life in a practical, workaday manner. CBN was in urgent need of $3 million worth of modern equipment that would allow us to broadcast with the power and quality needed if we were to do what the Lord had called us to do. With absolutely no worldly credentials or the support that

---

6See Ephesians 2:8–18.
7See Hebrews 4:14–16.
8Ephesians 2:4–7.
9See Numbers 6:24,25.

would normally be required to do business at this level, I began negotiations with one of the world's leading electronics manufacturers. There was no reason to expect a successful outcome.

But God had other plans. In the most remarkable, yet smooth and calm manner, I received total favor from this giant company and arranged for our equipment needs to be met for a period of years at the finest terms imaginable. Others in the industry were envious, for I had received every concession in price, down payment, and credit terms that it was possible to get.

You see, God had let His face shine upon us and was gracious to us. We had favor with Him in the invisible world, and since He ruled even the visible world that tried to ignore Him, He gave us favor there as well.

A Partnership

With those two truths of abundance and favor established, we are ready for the fact that God has entered into a partnership with redeemed man. He has given us the potential of cooperating with His Spirit in the whole work of the kingdom. Prayer is the link between finite man and the infinite purposes of God. In its ultimate sense, it consists of determining God's will and then doing it on earth. It does *not* consist merely of asking for what *we* want. To pray in the truest sense means to put our lives into total conformity with what God desires.

We begin this process by dropping our own preconceived ideas and entering His presence by grace to wait upon Him. Our thought should be: "Lord, what do *You* want? What are *You* doing?" As George Mueller, the great British man of faith, said, "Have no mind of your own in the matter."

The Lord's chastisement of the false prophets, recorded in the Book of Jeremiah, illustrates the importance of this. Warning the people against those prophets who were speaking visions of their own imaginations and not from the mouth of God, He asked: " 'But who has stood in the council of the LORD,/That he should see and hear His word?/Who has given heed to His word and listened?' "[10] They were to be alone with the Lord, to see and to hear what He was doing. They were not to put their own ideas first.

So it should be with us when we pray. We should stand in the Spirit in the invisible kingdom; there we will see and hear, and our role in the partnership can become active.

If we turn again to the account of Jesus and the fig tree as recorded in Mark's Gospel, which we touched on in chapter two, this becomes clear. We should recall that Jesus, discussing the power that withered the tree, said that the first thing required was "faith in God," absolute trust and confidence that He is God Almighty, unlimited and infinite. Implied was the fact that He speaks to His people, revealing what He is doing. Then Jesus said this:

For verily I say unto you, that whosoever shall say unto this mountain, Be thou removed, and be thou cast into the sea; and shall not doubt in his heart, but shall believe that those things which he saith shall come to pass; he shall have whatsoever he saith.[11]

If we fully believe God and have discerned His will, Christ said that we may translate that will from the invisible world to the visible by the spoken word. In short, God uses the spoken word to translate spiritual energy—sheer power—into the material.

The most vivid illustration, of course, was the creation of the world. God spoke to the void and said, " 'Let there be light.' "[12] and there was light. The same with the firmament and the waters

---

[10]Jeremiah 23:18.
[11]Mark 11:23,KJV.
[12]Genesis 1:3.

and the dry land; the same with everything that was created.[13] All things were made by the Word.[14] And that which was spoken was energized by the Spirit, moving upon the face of the waters,[15] shaping matter, which is itself energy, into God's predetermined patterns.

In like manner, our partnership with God is fulfilled when we speak His word in the power of the Holy Spirit. As Jesus taught: " 'Therefore I say unto you, What things soever ye desire, when ye pray, believe that ye receive them, and ye shall have them.' "[16] Thus He took us right back to where He began. Have faith in God, know who He is, know what He is doing, trust His favor upon us, participate with Him. What we say in His name should then come to pass.

The Missing Link

For the vast majority of Christians throughout history, the "speaking" has been the missing link between what we believe and what we do. We have lost the understanding of how God Almighty works, how His Son works, and how we are to work once we enter into the unobstructed view of God that Jesus provides in the kingdom.

The thing that clouds our view is sin. But once the sin is forgiven, we are to enter boldly into the throne room of grace and commune with God by the Spirit, who communicates with our spirit. It's a bit like tuning into a radio or television station. You get on the right frequency and you pick up a program. So it is

---

[13]See Genesis 1.
[14]See John 1:3.
[15]See Genesis 1:2.
[16]Mark 11:24, KJV.

with listening to the Lord. He is speaking constantly, but we are often on the wrong frequency.

Once He has spoken to us, we are to speak after Him. If we do, miracles occur. If we don't, usually nothing will happen. For, in the material world, God has chosen to enter into partnership with us, his colaborers, whom He is grooming for the perfect, visible establishment of His kingdom on earth.

Right now, in this life, He would have us stop cajoling and begging. He would have us live in the kingdom, in harmony with Him, receiving His thoughts by the Spirit. As the apostle Paul said, ". . . We have the mind of Christ."[17] So speak that mind, Jesus was saying in the fig tree episode. Speak His thoughts. Don't be afraid. Don't doubt. "For God has not given us a spirit of timidity, but of power and love and discipline."[18]

We must see that, by living in the kingdom now, we enter back into what man lost in the Garden of Eden. We return to the authority God gave us at the Creation. Like Adam, we hear the Lord's voice revealing the secrets of the world. And, as He speaks, we speak after Him in the manner of Ezekiel in his vision in the valley of dry bones.

Again He said to me, "Prophesy over these bones, and say to them, 'O dry bones, hear the word of the LORD.'"[19]

The prophet listened as the Lord said He intended to give the bones life, sinews, flesh, skin, and breath. Then it was Ezekiel's turn.

So *I prophesied* as I was commanded; and as *I prophesied*, there was a noise, and behold, a rattling; and the bones came together, bone to its bone. And I looked, and behold, sinews were on them, and flesh

---

[17]1 Corinthians 2:16.
[18]2 Timothy 1:7.
[19]Ezekiel 37:4.

grew, and skin covered them; but there was no breath in them. Then He said to me, "Prophesy to the breath, prophesy, son of man, and say to the breath, 'Thus says the LORD GOD, "Come from the four winds, O breath, and breathe on these slain, that they come to life."'" So I *prophesied* as He commanded me, and the breath came into them, and they came to life, and stood on their feet, an exceedingly great army.[20]

In this Old Testament episode, Ezekiel learned what I call the word of faith, which didn't receive full development until the New Testament was written. The lesson was this: Through our words, we translate the will of God in the invisible kingdom to the visible situation that confronts us. We speak to money, and it comes. We speak to storms, and they cease. We speak to crops, and they flourish.

Although I will discuss this miraculous phenomenon in detail later, the simple truth is that God's word, spoken into a situation, will perform His purpose: "So shall My word be which goes forth from My mouth;/It shall not return to Me empty,/Without accomplishing what I desire,/And without succeeding in the matter for which I sent it."[21]

The Way It Will Be

Some day, when the kingdom is fully manifested, the speaking will not be necessary. The thought will become the deed, as it is in heaven today.

On my television program, "The 700 Club," I did an interview with Dr. Richard E. Eby, a well-known California obstetrician and gynecologist, that illustrates the point vividly. In 1972, he said, he fell from a second-story balcony and split his skull. He

---

[20]Ezekiel 37:7–10.
[21]Isaiah 55:11.

65

told me that he died (whether for minutes or hours, he doesn't know) but miraculously returned to life and today is perfectly healthy and normal.

During the experience, Dr. Eby related, his spirit left his body and apparently went to heaven, or paradise. As one would expect, he found it to be a most beautiful place. At one stage he entered a field of flowers and as he walked along, he was overwhelmed by their beauty. "Wouldn't it be wonderful if I had a bunch and could smell them?" he thought. But as he started to bend over, he looked at his hand, and it was already full of flowers.

At another point, he was thinking how good it would be to go to a distant valley and, behold, he was there.

As a scientific man, he naturally analyzed these experiences carefully and concluded that in heaven the mere thought produces the action. As the psalmist declared: "Delight yourself in the LORD;/And He will give you the desires of your heart."[22]

In heaven, Dr. Eby was delighting himself in the Lord, doing His perfect will, and the yearnings of his heart were immediately fulfilled. He didn't have to speak them. On earth a translation is required, but not so in the ultimate kingdom. One day we will not need telephones, mass transit, or computers as the speed of thought eclipses the speed of light. But now we need the spoken word.

What Is Faith?

As we have emphasized several times, the covering statement for the entire matter of how the kingdom works is "Have faith in God." Faith governs all. But it is frequently misunderstood.

The Bible says bluntly:

---

[22]Psalm 37:4.

Now faith is the assurance of things hoped for, the conviction of things not seen. For by it the men of old gained approval. By faith we understand that the worlds were prepared by the word of God, so that what is seen was not made out of things which are visible. . . . And without faith it is impossible to please Him, for he who comes to God must believe that He is, and that He is a rewarder of those who seek Him.[23]

The Living Bible's paraphrase is helpful:

What is Faith? It is the confident assurance that something we want is going to happen. It is the certainty that what we hope for is waiting for us, even though we cannot see it up ahead. . . .[24]

Said another way, faith is the title deed to things we can't see. When we buy property, we meet with the seller and papers are drawn up. We receive a deed and it says we own a stated piece of property. The minute it is signed, we own the property. We don't have to go to it; we don't have to see it. It's ours. We have a title deed.

The same with faith. We have a title deed to what God has promised. Our role is to believe in our hearts that it has been accomplished, according to what God has given us the deed to, and then to speak it. We can't force it. We can't sit around a room with a group and work it up. We can receive it only from God. The Bible says: "So then faith cometh by hearing, and hearing by the word of God."[25]

We hear the Lord's Word; it builds in our hearts, and the light goes on. "It's mine!" Deep down inside, there will be no doubt. That is what the Lord meant when He referred in the fig tree episode to the one who speaks to the mountain and "does not

---

[23]Hebrews 11:1–3,6.
[24]Hebrews 11:1, TLB.
[25]Romans 10:17, KJV.

doubt in his heart." The mountain will move if the Lord has spoken.

The Bible also cautions about double-mindedness:

. . . let him ask in faith without any doubting, for the one who doubts is like the surf of the sea driven and tossed by the wind. For let not that man expect that he will receive anything from the Lord, being a double-minded man, unstable in all his ways.[26]

There can be no equivocating, no going back and forth. So many of us hear something from the Lord, we believe it briefly, but the wind blows and the storm pounds and our faith in what God said vanishes like the mist. We need to counter by speaking the word God has given and then simply accepting it.

I must add a word, however, to drive home a subtle point. Our faith throughout all of this must be in the Lord—"have faith in God," Jesus said—and not in our ability, our stubborn strength. Our faith is not to be *in our faith:* "Trust in the LORD with all your heart,/And do not lean on your own understanding."[27]

For the Lord, while structuring most of His dealings with man around the point of faith, made plain that His insistence on faith was not quantitative, but qualitative. He said we would move mountains if we had faith the size of a mustard seed.[28] We don't need a mountain of faith to move a mountain of dirt or even a mountain of world problems.

The object and reality of the faith are the issues. We don't need stubbornness, but confidence.

. . . this is the confidence which we have before Him, that, if we ask anything according to His will, He hears us. And if we know that He hears us in whatever we ask, we know that we have the requests which we have asked from Him.[29]

---

[26]James 1:6–8.
[27]Proverbs 3:5.
[28]See Matthew 17:20.
[29]1 John 5:14,15.

The Importance of Right Thinking

We begin to see that in the kingdom:
—Spirit controls matter.
—Lesser authority yields to greater authority.
—The mind is the ultimate conduit of the spirit.
—Speech is the intermediate conduit between spirit and matter and between greater and lesser authority.

That which the writers of the many "success" books call "positive mental attitude," or PMA, is indeed important. Because our minds are the agents our spirits use in influencing the world around us, it is patently clear that negative attitudes can vitiate our most valiant attempts. Conversely, positive thinking will more often than not lead to successful action.

Unfortunately, such people as Napoleon Hill, who wrote *Think and Grow Rich,* have gleaned only a few of the truths of the kingdom of God. They try to gain the kingdom without submitting themselves to the King.

Some of the metaphysical principles of the kingdom, taken by themselves, can produce fantastic temporal benefits. But without the lordship of Jesus, these benefits are both transitory and harmful. In fact, many of the advocates of mind over matter ultimately end in hellish spiritism. " 'What will a man be profited, if he gains the whole world, and forfeits his soul? . . .' "[30]

Many sincere followers of Jesus Christ destroy their effectiveness in this world because they do not understand the laws of spiritual authority and the way this authority is transmitted. They especially are not aware of the power of what they say.

Solomon wrote: "From the fruit of a man's mouth he enjoys good. . . ."[31] In other words, when you confess blessing, favor, victory, and success, those things will come to you.

---

[30]Matthew 16:26.
[31]Proverbs 13:2

69

But the majority of Christians ignore this truth. "How do you feel?" we ask someone.

"I feel terrible," he replies, not realizing he has commanded his body to be sick.

"Can you do it?" we ask.

"I can't do that," he replies, not knowing he has limited God and himself by his words.

"I can't get out of debt," someone says. He has just commanded his debt to continue.

We call such negative assertions "realistic appraisals" of the situation. But they aren't realistic, for they ignore the power of God, the authority of the invisible world of the spirit, and the grant of power made by God to His children.

A much more realistic assertion was made by the apostle Paul when he boldly declared: "I can do all things through Him who strengthens me."[32]

Pettiness, overemphasis on minutiae, fear of failure, constant complaining, murmuring—all inhibit the realization of kingdom conditions. As a man thinks in his heart, so he is.[33]

Many athletes and men of physical accomplishment have realized this principle. Ben Hogan, the golfer, was one. As he approached a shot, in his mind's eye he would see himself swinging the club and the ball traveling in a perfect arc, landing in a particular spot. He set the pattern in his mind. And then he followed through with his body. His success was spectacular.

The same has been true with runners and jumpers. God has given us minds and bodies that work that way. Our bodies will obey our minds, for the most part. Added to that is the fact that our spirits can be in touch with God. Now if our spirits govern our minds and our minds govern our bodies, then God in the invisible world governs us in the visible world.

---

[32]Philippians 4:13.
[33]See Proverbs 23:7, KJV.

At the same time, the Lord has called for us to be honest and truthful in the innermost being,[34] so we are not to delude ourselves and to say something is true when it is not. We are not to engage in superstition or silliness. We merely are to have confidence that with Him all things are possible.

Perhaps the most dramatic example of proper thinking, speaking, and doing came to my attention through "The 700 Club." It involved Leslie, May, and Joe Lemke and an extraordinary true-life story of love.

The story began in 1952 when May, a nurse-governess with a reputation for unusual ability with children, was asked to take care of a six-month-old baby named Leslie who was retarded, who had cerebral palsy, and whose eyes had been removed because they were diseased. Leslie was not expected to live long.

The Lord gave May a great love for Leslie, and she began to treat him like a normal baby. She taught him to feed from a nursing bottle by making loud sucking noises against his cheek. Soon she gave up everything else to take care of the child. "I have a job to do for Jesus now," she said, "and I'm going to do it."

By the time he was ten, Leslie could move only a hand and friends advised May that she was wasting her time. But she refused to concede. "I'm doing something for an innocent boy who will be something some day," she said. "I believe in God, and He will do it."

She carried the boy around and spoke her love into his ear, holding him and squeezing him continuing to treat him like a normal child. Eventually he learned to stand by holding onto a fence, and then to walk by following it.

Throughout it all, May prayed constantly for Leslie. Before long, she added a thought to her petitions, repeating it to the Lord several times a day: "Dear Lord, the Bible says you gave

---

[34]See Psalm 51:6.

each of us a talent. Please help me find the talent in this poor boy who lies there most of the day and does nothing."

May noticed that the boy seemed to respond to musical sounds like the plucking of a string or a cord. So she and her husband, Joe, bought a piano; and she played him all kinds of music, using the radio and records. Leslie listened for hours, seemingly in deep concentration.

After four years of praying for the boy's "talent" to be revealed, May and Joe were awakened at 3:00 A.M. one night by the sound of piano music. They found Leslie sitting at the piano playing beautifully, like a trained musician. He was sixteen years old.

Over the next ten years, the boy learned dozens of songs—classical, popular, jazz—and has even learned to sing with the playing. His talent was fully manifested through May's constant love and confession that nothing is impossible with God. She discerned God's purpose and spoke it into being, thoroughly rejecting negativism.

A Necessary Ingredient

Perhaps history's biggest roadblock to effective demonstration of the invisible kingdom is found in negativism. For in the final analysis, it reveals the absence of *unity*, about which I will have more to say in conjunction with other principles. But at this point, we need to see that the kingdom of God works through the phenomenon of harmony.

To begin with, entrance into the kingdom, totally dependent upon grace and not upon any kind of status or merit, immediately establishes a basic equality among people. No one can say, "I've earned a better place than you." Growing from that logically is a new relationship between individuals. It is one based on the will of the Father, surpassing existing national, racial, familial, or church relationships. The Lord Jesus was precise on this: " '. . . whoever does the will of My Father who is in heaven, he is My brother and sister and mother.' "[35]

That statement transcended the Lord's own family relationships, and it transcends ours. The kingdom thus is a family. Jesus is our elder brother; His Father is our father. That cuts across all lines. My mother can be a black woman who does the will of the Father. My brother can be a Chinese who does likewise, or a Jew, or an Arab.

How we need to see this! All strife and turmoil in the world can be eliminated simply by its fulfillment. The Middle East can be at peace. Latin America can be at peace. The aged and the young can be at peace.

This wholly unique concept of love and family relationships can produce that which has escaped man's grasp from the beginning. But peace will not be the only fruit of such transferal of kingdom life to this world. Paul the apostle wrote of the "fruit of the Spirit" that would grow in a climate of unity—"love, joy, peace, patience, kindness, goodness, faithfulness, gentleness, self-control."[36] Against such characteristics there is no law, Paul added. None is needed.

The Scripture's classic illustration of the transfer of kingdom power to the visible world when there is unity comes in a well-known but underutilized portion of Matthew's Gospel.

"Again I say to you, that if two of you agree on earth about anything that they may ask, it shall be done for them by My Father who is in heaven. "For where two or three have gathered together in My name, there I am in their midst."[37]

---

[35]Matthew 12:50.
[36]Galatians 5:22,23.
[37]Matthew 18:19,20.

73

The full implication of the point is that when there is no unity of purpose, no crossover of barriers, then the power is not activated.

Prospects for Improvement

I am confident that we will see the kingdom of God working more in the visible world as the Lord continues to bring people to Himself. Should the world experience the great revival of faith in Jesus Christ that I am expecting, then it would be reasonable to see an increase in the exercise of these truths of the kingdom. This, I am sure, will enable the world to transcend many of the limitations we are experiencing now.

For example, it is clear that we are going to run out of fossil fuels, even though at times we experience some relief in the oil and gas shortage. We can't keep burning limited resources forever. But we have some very big oceans, and they contain hydrogen. Sooner or later, God may give to one or more of His people a concept for running cars on such water. He will simply allow a peek into the invisible world to see His purpose. Then a faithful one will speak and act according to the revelation, and the concept will take life.

I believe we can expect this in the area of building materials, perhaps to replace steel and other items in short supply. I am sure there will be foodstuffs we haven't dreamed of, perhaps new living space to accommodate vast populations. The limits are not found in what we see, feel, and taste. They are in our hearts and our willingness to stand in that place where we have an unclouded view of what the Lord is doing.

Thoughts like these invariably cause concern about whether someone who is not prospering or indeed is suffering in slums and poverty is violating the truths of the kingdom. Such questions must not be dismissed hastily. For there is suffering in the world and seemingly many Christians are living short of the ideals we are discussing and are in great distress.

What can we say? I am convinced that if a person is *continuously* in sickness, poverty, or other physical and mental straits, then he is missing the truths of the kingdom. He has either failed to grasp the points we have been making in this chapter about the operation of the kingdom or is not living according to the major principles we will be exploring. He has missed the prosperity I believe the Scripture promises.

True, there is suffering, even in God's will, but as with the cross of Christ, it doesn't last forever.

It is important, however, that we not try to equate scriptural prosperity with riches. We are speaking of the Lord's blessing, not great material wealth. Some people are not capable of handling money or other wealth. Some would be destroyed by pride. So God prospers according to His wisdom, according to the true need of those involved.

Nonetheless, I believe Christians can escape any ghetto to which they have been confined, real or imagined. God will make a way. He will provide methods with which to reverse conditions and attitudes. Shortage will turn to abundance, hostility to favor.

As for tragedy and seemingly inevitable mishap, the Bible says:

The steps of a good man are ordered by the LORD: and he delighteth in his way. Though he fall down, *he shall not be utterly cast down:* for the LORD upholdeth him with his hand.[38]

Furthermore, it says the wicked will try to harm the righteous, but "the LORD will not leave him in his hand."[39] There may be difficult days and even stumbling, but God's arm will be there to deliver the faithful.

---

[38]Psalm 37:23,24, KJV.
[39]Psalm 37:33.

75

FIVE

PROGRESSIVE HAPPINESS

As we have seen, the kingdom of heaven exists now, here. Although it is spiritual and invisible, it governs the material and visible. It is inhabited by people who have been born again spiritually. It operates in a specified manner.

Now we see that it also has a constitution, a system of fundamental principles and virtues to determine the quality and conduct of life. That constitution is contained in what has come to be known as the Sermon on the Mount, presented by Jesus quite early in His public ministry, probably within the first year.

It clearly sums up a new way of life. It demands an inner revolution of attitude and outlook. It turns ordinary ideas upside down. It sets the stage for a new world order.

This constitution has a preamble. We label its eight points as the Beatitudes, which is fitting since they truly do guarantee "blessedness" or "happiness." Happy are those who live by them.

They also show us a lot about the nature of God, the one ruling the kingdom.

Complemented by principles and virtues set forth throughout Scripture, they provide the underpinning and framework for real life, even during a time of transition from the old, discredited order into the emerging future.

As we explore these well-known, yet still-alien words, we should peer between and behind them to perceive the Lord Himself. For the Beatitudes demonstrate the nature of God in a sweeping, foundational way.

We should start by remembering that God's name, Yahweh, is no mere label but is significant of the real personality of the one bearing it. It stems from the Hebrew word for "to be," and some authorities believe it may be the so-called hiph'il tense, which would mean "He who causes everything to be."

At any rate, He revealed Himself to the covenant people as I AM.[1] It was almost like a blank check. God said, "I am _____," and His people were to fill in the blank according to their need. If they needed peace, He was Jehovah-shalom—"I am your peace."[2] If they needed victory, He was Jehovah-nissi—"I am your banner, your victory."[3] If they needed help of any kind, as Abraham so desperately did when he was being tested regarding his son, Isaac, then He was Jehovah-jireh—"I am your provider."[4]

The point we should remember, which is the one the Beatitudes demonstrate so simply, is that God revealed Himself, His nature, His power and His will at the point of the need. The people had to recognize and acknowledge their need.

This is an overriding lesson of the Beatitudes, which is essen-

---

[1]See Exodus 3:14.
[2]See Judges 6:24.
[3]See Exodus 17:15.
[4]See Genesis 22:14

77 🐟

tial to life in the kingdom. The one who feels he has need of nothing *will receive nothing*. He will never experience the full name and nature of God. He will never know His peace and comfort; he will never know His victory; he will never know His provision of every need of life. Indeed, he will never know His salvation and experience the name God gave to His Son—Jesus, which means "I Am Salvation."

No, the self-sufficient, the self-righteous will not experience the kingdom of heaven. The void within them will not be filled if they do not cry out, "God Almighty, come and meet the deepest need in my life."

Let's look at the Beatitudes themselves,[5] taking note of their progressive nature in the working of an individual's life.

Spiritual Beggars

"Blessed are the poor in spirit, for theirs is the kingdom of heaven."

As with each of the points, the Lord began with a word that is preserved for us in the New Testament as *makarios* which we render usually as "blessed" or "happy." Therefore, each of the points contains a guideline to happiness, which our world desperately craves.

"Happy are the poor in spirit." What a contradiction this seems! But upon closer examination it becomes clear. First we must understand that the Lord meant more than merely "poor." His words conveyed the meaning "beggarly." Happy are the beggars in spirit, the spiritual beggars, those who know they are needy and are not afraid to say so, as we noted above.

The Lord's teaching at another time made the point most dramatically. Contrasting a shame-stricken publican (or tax-

---

[5]See Matthew 5:3–12.

gatherer) with a proud Pharisee, He revealed a man who was poor in spirit.

"And the publican, standing afar off, would not lift up so much as his eyes unto heaven, but smote upon his breast, saying, God be merciful to me a sinner. I tell you, this man went down to his house justified rather than the other: for every one that exalteth himself shall be abased; and he that humbleth himself shall be exalted."[6]

He was exalted right into the kingdom, into perfect happiness. He had been empty, but he was filled, simply because he was ready to acknowledge that he needed God and was willing to beg for help. The kingdom was his, right then—"theirs *is* the kingdom." He had taken the first step in the progression demonstrated in the Beatitudes.

The Intercessors

"Blessed are those who mourn, for they shall be comforted."

This contradiction seems more extreme than the first. Happy are those who mourn. How can it be?

We find help from the writings of Paul, in which he told of a "godly sorrow" that works repentance.[7] This is what Jesus was pointing to. For "repentance" means "afterthought" or "reconsideration." A man is to be repentant, to have an afterthought, to reconsider. He is to be sorry for his sins; he is never to be self-satisfied. As the psalmist wrote:

The sacrifices of God are a broken spirit;
A broken and contrite heart, O God, Thou wilt not despise.[8]

6Luke 18:13,14, KJV.
72 Corinthians 7:10, KJV.
8Psalm 51:17.

So the Lord's message in this second Beatitude was, in essence, "if you want the comfort of God surrounding you, you must come to a place where you mourn for your sins." But He pressed it beyond that; He wanted us to mourn for the sins of people around us, too. The world does not want to mourn; it wants to laugh all the time. But rather than thumbing our noses at the world, we are to mourn, to hurt, to cry out for the lost.

We have the biblical account of Lot in Sodom and Gomorrah, where greed, drunkenness, homosexuality, and corruption were rampant. Lot, a "righteous man," was not merely angered by the filthy deeds of the wicked; he was "vexed" and "tormented" in his soul.[9] He mourned over their deeds. And God comforted him by sending angels to preserve him when those cities were destroyed.[10]

Do you see the progression? The kingdom becomes ours; we are in it. Immediately, the magnitude of our sin falls upon us, even though the Lord has forgiven us. In quick succession, we then see the sin of others—our relatives and friends who are not saved, indeed, the whole world. We are burdened with concern for others. We mourn. We become intercessors.

A philosophy has swept the earth that says, in effect, "I'm OK; you're OK." Without Jesus' salvation there is no room in His kingdom for such thinking. Complacency is an abomination. We have only to recall the lesson He gave when speaking of His second coming. It will be just like the days of Noah, He said.

"For as in those days which were before the flood they were eating and drinking, they were marrying and giving in marriage, until the day that Noah entered the ark, and they did not understand until the flood came and took them all away, so shall the coming of the Son of Man be."[11]

---

[9] 2 Peter 2:6–8, KJV and NASB.
[10] See Genesis 19:1–26.
[11] Matthew 24:38,39.

He deplored the people's complacency over the condition of the world. In the kingdom, this must give way to concern and mourning. Then we can expect the fulfillment of Jeremiah's prophecy: " '. . . For I will turn their mourning into joy,/And will comfort them, and give them joy for their sorrow.' "[12]

A Matter of Control

"Blessed are the meek, for they shall inherit the earth."

This next step in the progression is one of the most misunderstood verses in the Bible. Conjuring up images of the famous cartoon character Caspar Milquetoast, it has convinced many that Jesus wanted His people to be dull, obsequious, spineless, and stupid. This, of course, runs contrary to everything we find about the men and women of God on the pages of Scripture. They were strong, vocal, and often brilliant.

Our problem has been with the word "meek." It *does* mean "humble" and "gentle," even "docile." But the definition cannot stop there. Biblical meekness does not call for the abject surrender of one's character or personal integrity. It calls for a total yielding of the reins of life from one's own hands to God's hands. But it doesn't stop there either. The meek exercise discipline, which results in their being kept continuously under God's control.

Thus, a meek man is a disciplined man who is under the control of God. He is like Moses, a strong, bold leader who at the same time was described as the meekest man on earth.[13] Having seen his sin and that of others, the meek person takes the next

---

12Jeremiah 31:13.
13See Numbers 12:3, KJV.

step and places himself under God's control and discipline. He serves God. But, remember, God will not seize control. He will govern a life only if it is constantly yielded to Him, and that requires constant discipline. God is not interested in building robots.

Happy is the man who is under control—of God and of himself. Earlier I mentioned Paul's reminder to his beloved Timothy that they had received a spirit of "power and love and *discipline* [or self-control]," not of "timidity."[14] This is what the Lord was talking about. One with this virtue will inherit the earth.

So often Christians have been misled into thinking that once they are born again, nothing is required. This, as we will see, is damaging. The Lord and all those who wrote of Him made clear that rebirth was only the beginning, to be followed by discipline, work, and suffering. Obviously the drunk, the drug addict, the lustful, the slothful do not have the discipline to rule the earth and to correct its evils. No, it is for the meek, the disciplined— those who are controlled by God, who follow His Son, who struggle. Remember these powerful words: " '. . . from the days of John the Baptist until now the kingdom of heaven suffers violence, and violent men take it by force.' "[15] Zealous men force their way in. That's what it means. Though the Milquetoasts fall by the wayside, God's meek men and women will inherit the earth.

A Work of the Spirit

"Blessed are those who hunger and thirst for righteousness, for they shall be satisfied [filled]."

---

[14]2 Timothy 1:7.
[15]Matthew 11:12.

God is righteousness. To be righteous is to be Godlike. Jesus said we should hunger and thirst after righteousness. It is a free gift,[16] but we must seek it. We should desire in every fiber to be Godlike in nature. For such can be ours. According to the Bible, God planted the Spirit of His Son within us when we received Him, not being satisfied that we merely be adopted children, but that we also have Christ's very nature *within* us.[17] We, setting our life's course in pursuit of Him, must yearn for this nature, this righteousness and holiness, to flood us. Having had the righteousness of Jesus *imputed* to us, we now should desire to have that righteousness *imparted* to us, actually living it out. If we remain unrighteous, the Bible says, we will miss the kingdom.

Or do you not know that the unrighteous shall not inherit the kingdom of God? Do not be deceived; neither fornicators, nor idolaters, not adulterers, nor effeminate, nor homosexuals, nor thieves, nor the covetous, nor drunkards, nor revilers, nor swindlers, shall inherit the kingdom of God.[18]

"I want to know more of God"—that should be our cry. "I want His Spirit to possess more of me. I want to be more effective. I want to see His kingdom come on earth."

With that cry of hunger and thirst for God, for more of His power, we in fact are crying out for an anointing of the Holy Spirit for service, which the Bible calls baptism in the Holy Spirit. This actually fulfills the next step in the progression of development revealed in the Beatitudes, providing an empowerment for serving God.

Jesus described it this way: " '. . . you shall receive power when the Holy Spirit has come upon you; and you shall be My witnesses both in Jerusalem, and in all Judea and Samaria, and

---

16See Romans 5:17.
17See Galatians 4:4–7; 2 Peter 1:3,4.
181 Corinthians 6:9,10.

even to the remotest part of the earth.' "[19] You will indeed be effective—being filled with the miraculous power of God Himself—simply because you hungered and thirsted for Him.

Yes, Jesus said, you will be filled and satisfied. Interestingly, the Greek word that we translate "filled" is *chortazo*,[20] which carries the implication of "gorged." We won't merely have a little, the Lord said; we will be gorged with righteousness, power, and everything good in the kingdom.

This obviously is the perfect fulfillment of " 'seek, and you will find' "[21]

The Flow of Mercy

"Blessed are the merciful, for they shall receive mercy."

Most of us grasp this one, but we may fall short in seeing its magnitude.

The root Greek word for mercy is *eleos*, containing the sense of compassion and tenderness, of kindness and beneficence. It flows from the greater to the lesser: God is merciful to man; a wealthy man is merciful to a poorer man.

Thus we see a further progression in the Beatitudes. We begin to think toward men as God thinks toward us, extending our work out into the world. Having received mercy from One greater than we are, we are to give mercy to those we are in a position to favor.

Although our motivation should be purer than this, the fact is

---

[19]Acts 1:8.
[20]Matthew 5:6.
[21]Luke 11:9

that as we show compassion to someone below us, there is always someone upstream to do the same for us—either men or God Himself. Behind this is a broader law that we will examine at greater length.

The Ultimate Happiness

"Blessed are the pure in heart, for they shall see God."

From the Middle Ages came the idea that "the highest good," the *summum bonum*, was the "beatific vision." The ultimate happiness was to see God. There could be nothing greater. It was its own reward—an end, not a means.

In this Beatitude, Jesus showed the way for the fulfillment of that truth, elevating to its climax the progression of experience we have observed in these teachings.

If the highest good, the supreme happiness, is to see God—and it is—then purity in heart is required. Again, we grasp this simple statement rather quickly, but frequently its greatness passes over our heads.

In the Bible the word "pure" often means clean and untainted, but it is also used to describe gold that is without alloy or unadulterated. So the Lord was saying more than "blessed are those who have clean hearts." He was additionally saying "blessed are those whose hearts are single and undivided, whose devotion is without mixture."

As for the word "heart," it means the center of our being, the core of our spirituality and deepest motivations. It is the real person.

It is not uncommon for people to want God, at least part of the time or with part of themselves, while at the same time wanting money and fame and all the world has to give. That won't do if you want to see God and receive the ultimate happiness, Jesus said.

Again, we need to see the insistence on unity and wholeness that filled the Lord's ministry. If your eye is unclear or dark, then your whole body will be full of darkness, He said, adding: " 'No one can serve two masters; for either he will hate the one and love the other, or he will hold to one and despise the other. You cannot serve God and mammon.' "22

We must focus on heaven or on earth. If it is the former, we will find the highest good.

The Way of Inheritance

"Blessed are the peacemakers, for they shall be called sons of God."

Most of us would indeed be happy were we the children of a reigning monarch with power to act in his name and eventually to rule. Well, that can be the case, and the monarch is known as the "King of Kings"23 whose realm is all of creation.

Now a child of God is an heir of God,24 the recipient of authority, possession, wealth, and even the kingdom itself. In short, he is the inheritor of everything that exists.

But, Jesus said, to progress to that status you must be a "peacemaker." And that is one who stops conflict and war.

The Lord Himself was the unique peacemaker, bringing peace between man and God.25 In His name we are to do the same. We are to be going throughout the earth saying to all men, "Your sins are pardoned. You can be reconciled to God." As Paul taught:

22Matthew 6:24.
23Revelation 19:16.
24See Romans 8:17.
25See Romans 5:1.

Now all these things are from God, who reconciled us to Himself through Christ, and gave us the ministry of reconciliation, namely, that God was in Christ reconciling the world to Himself, not counting their trespasses against them, and He has committed to us the word of reconciliation. Therefore, we are ambassadors for Christ, as though God were entreating through us; we beg you on behalf of Christ, be reconciled to God.[26]

Indeed, we as peacemakers should be *begging* people to accept that which God has already done, since reconciliation is a two-way street requiring a response from both parties. For the world still echoes with the song of the heavenly host on a quiet night two thousand years ago: " 'peace, good will toward men.' "[27] Each Christmas Eve, even the hardest hearts quiver at the prospect. Man craves God and peace from his deepest recesses.

However, the sons of God, the peacemakers, do not stop at the point of peace with God. They work for peace between men. They themselves are not warriors, and they counsel others to stop fighting among themselves. Their goal is peace among individuals and among nations as they constantly strive to bring conflicting groups together and seek harmony and love, not at the expense of godly principle, but through godly relationships.

These will be blessed, for they do the will and the work of the Father, as sons and daughters. They will mature as heirs, and they will inherit their Father's estate, the kingdom.

Persecution Will Come

"Blessed are those who have been persecuted for the sake of righteousness, for theirs is the kingdom of heaven.

---

[26]2 Corinthians 5:18–20.
[27]Luke 2:14, KJV.

"Blessed are you when men cast insults at you, and persecute you, and say all kinds of evil against you falsely, on account of Me."[28]

A new world order is near. It is called the eternal kingdom of heaven, to be brought about by God Almighty. Only certain people will live in it. And it is the Lord's intention that those people practice living in it right now, doing His will and experiencing the blessings at this time.

As they do so, however—bringing every thought captive and exercising the authority of the kingdom—they will become visible for who they are, and opposition will mount. Abuse will come. It came to Jesus; it came to the early saints.

But, this Beatitude says, they will be happy as they continue in their remarkable realm. Indeed, wrote the apostle Peter, they will be experiencing genuine maturity: "If you are reviled for the name of Christ, you are blessed, because *the Spirit of glory and of God rests upon you.*"[29] The blessing can hardly be greater than that in this life.

Many people innocently ask, "But why would anyone want to persecute people if they're loving and kind?"

The answer lies deep in the innermost parts of unregenerate man. He is offended by the beauty of others, by their brightness, their happiness, their prosperity. He prefers a dark, worried countenance to a clear, carefree one. He simply loves darkness more than light, which is a specific disclosure of Scripture.[30]

The Bible says those who are following Christ bear a fragrance that is distinguishable both to the believer and the unbeliever. To one, it is the sweet aroma of life; to the other, the stench of death.[31] Such a person produces either appreciation or offense. The offense has at times turned to rage and persecution.

---

[28]Matthew 5:10,11.
[29]1 Peter 4:14.
[30]See John 3:19.
[31]See 2 Corinthians 2:15,16.

The Greek root behind the word we translate "persecute" means "to pursue," in the manner one would chase a fox or rabbit in a hunt, and pursuit is sometimes what results from the world's rage and persecution. "We must drive them from our midst," people roar. "We must search them out and destroy them." Before his conversion, Paul the apostle did the same thing to the Christians as his offense turned to fury.[32]

But whether it be rage or merely rudeness, Jesus said we would be happy. "When men lie about you, when they curse you, when they throw you into prison because you remind them of God," He said, "be glad, rejoice, jump up and down, for the kingdom is yours. It is already yours."

The progression has reached fullness.

---

[32]See Acts 8:3.

SIX

UPSIDE DOWN

From the constitution of the kingdom of God, which so clearly reverses normal world thinking, we see that one virtue comes ahead of all others in the invisible realm. It is humility.

How can humility underlie happiness, prosperity, and fulfillment?

In my own case, the deep significance of this virtue unfolded in my constant search for wisdom from God. For, as we will see, wisdom and humility are thoroughly intertwined.

At one point, the following words sprang to life in my spirit: " '. . . God *resisteth* the proud, but giveth grace unto the humble.' "[1] The power of those words is devastating if you trace the logic. Not only does God help those with genuine humility, but also He actively *opposes* those who are proud.

---

[1] James 4:6, KJV.

Of course, the definition of humble that is easiest for most of us to grasp is that it is the opposite of proud. Most of us seem to know what pride is. God insists that we be the very opposite if we are to receive His favor and blessing; otherwise He is against us.

Thus it became clear to me that if we desire to live in the kingdom of God, to receive God's favor, we must make humility the number one virtue. It is foundational.

Jesus, the very Son of God, existing in the form of God, took on the likeness of man without diminishing His deity and "humbled Himself by becoming obedient to the point of death, even death on a cross."[2] And His Father *favored* that humility in this manner. "Therefore also God highly *exalted* Him, and bestowed on Him the name which is above every name. . . ."[3]

The Old Testament prepares us for such a consequence with words like: "The reward of humility and the fear of the LORD/ Are riches, honor and life."[4]

Those humble before God, obedient and reverent toward Him and His will, are the victorious ones, the ones elevated to the rewards that the world scrambles after—riches, honor, life. Just consider the competition, the greed, the worry, the abuse, the killing expended in the race for those benefits. People worldwide want (1) enough to live on, (2) recognition and approval of what they do, and (3) good health and long life. To the humble and obedient, these blessings come naturally.

The path of the proud is perfectly clear from Scripture, for without question pride is the greatest sin there is in the eyes of God. It thwarts His goodness toward man.

The proud man says, "I'll do it my way. I'm sufficient. I can control my destiny. I'm the captain of my soul, the master of my fate." There is nothing spiritually beggarly about him, nothing

---

[2]Philippians 2:8.
[3]Philippians 2:9.
[4]Proverbs 22:4.

regretful about his inner condition, nothing hungering to be Godlike. In short, he lacks humility; and he receives nothing from the Lord, as we saw in discussing God's nature. His rewards, which are from men, are like vapor; they vanish suddenly, imperceptibly. For the wisdom of the Scripture says, "Pride goes before destruction/And a haughty spirit before stumbling."[5]

Where there is pride, there will always be a fall. It is inevitable. We see it all about us, on a large scale and on small. Nations and individuals are slipping. They become arrogant; they cut off advice from old and respected friends; they go alone, and they fall.

As we strive to look into the invisible world to see God, to hear what He is saying, it is essential that we always bear in mind that our knowledge of that world comes primarily through His disclosure. *He* must reveal. Otherwise, we cannot see. Recollection of that should keep us humble, even though our confidence rests in the fact that He said He would be found by those who diligently seek Him.[6] The proud, however, cannot bring themselves to seek, for that requires coming in from a lower position; and they have been conditioned otherwise.

Solomon Was Right

As I said, humility is closely entwined with wisdom, which was the object of my diligent search years ago. I had been impressed with Solomon's reply to the Lord's offer one night following King David's death, " 'Ask what I shall give you' "[7]

Can you imagine how most of us would have replied? But the Bible shows that Solomon revealed great humility in even ap-

---

[5]Proverbs 16:18.
[6]See Jeremiah 29:13,14.
[7]2 Chronicles 1:7.

proaching God, describing himself as a little child. " '. . . I do not know how to go out or come in,' " he said.[8] " 'Give me now wisdom and knowledge . . . for who can rule this great people of Thine?' "[9]

The Lord's response laid bare the pattern prevailing in the kingdom of heaven.

". . . Because you had this in mind, and did not ask for riches, wealth, or honor, or the life of those who hate you, nor have you even asked for long life, but you have asked for yourself wisdom and knowledge, that you may rule My people, over whom I have made you king, wisdom and knowledge have been granted to you. And I will give you riches and wealth and honor, such as none of the kings who were before you possessed, nor those who will come after you."[10]

Echoing throughout were the words of Christ centuries later. "Seek first His kingdom and His righteousness; and all these things shall be added to you."[11]

I have become convinced that wisdom is the key to the secrets of the kingdom of God. It leads to favor. But the starting point is humility, as Solomon knew. For humility reveals fear of, or reverence for, the Lord.

The Book of Proverbs reveals the next step: "The fear of the LORD is the beginning of wisdom,/And the knowledge of the Holy One is understanding."[12]

The cycle is complete—from humility, to fear of the Lord, to wisdom, to knowledge of the Holy One.

Wisdom, or spiritual understanding, *is* knowledge of the Holy

---

[8]1 Kings 3:7.
[9]2 Chronicles 1:10.
[10]2 Chronicles 1:11,12.
[11]Matthew 6:33.
[12]Proverbs 9:10.

One. And that is what we are seeking—knowledge of God, knowledge of His will and purpose, knowledge of the invisible world and how it works, knowledge of how to reach into it and bring its blessing and prosperity into our visible world.

In its ultimate sense, wisdom is understanding that an action taken today will be proven in the future to have been a correct one. And God provides that understanding.

To the people of Israel, God presented a body of Law that was to be their wisdom, an external expression of His will. If they followed those rules and principles in their society, then many years later people would look back and say they had acted wisely. Unfortunately, they were inconsistent and often improperly motivated, and God's wisdom was not fully realized in their lives.

Through the incarnation of Christ and the coming of the Holy Spirit to dwell within believers, the wisdom of God took on an internal expression, with which we are now dealing. Obviously, like the Israelites, we have not been consistent or sincere in all of our efforts to manifest it.

But this wisdom from God is still available. Knowing that He governs all things, present and future, we can approach Him with pure hearts and say: "Show me how to run my life. Show me how the world works. Show me Your ways, Your principles, for running this enormously complex universe. I want to conform to what You do, to Your will, Your purpose, Your plan."

At that point we are seeking truth, and He will grant us wisdom for that. His entire purpose is to have us conform to truth. His wisdom will come; His principles will work. We will act, and the future will bear us out. People will say, "My, wasn't that man wise? Where did he get such wisdom?"

And all the while, it came from God.

Lesson From the Garden

It is helpful to recognize that the entire point of conflict in the Garden of Eden came from God's attempt to teach Adam and Eve wisdom. It was not that God wanted to prevent them from obtaining knowledge by forbidding them to eat from the tree of the knowledge of good and evil. His purpose was that they would gain wisdom by obeying Him. Day after day they were to pass that tree, saying, "If I eat the fruit from there, that will be evil; if I refrain from eating it, that will be good." They were to learn good and evil simply from having that tree in their midst.

We know that they ate, did evil, and failed to obtain what God intended. For good is doing what God wants; it reveals wisdom. Evil is doing what He does not want; it reveals foolishness.

God was, and still is, looking for people who will do what He wants, people with wisdom, that He may enter into their lives, their visible world, and favor them. No problem, no shortage, no crisis is beyond His ability.

But instead He encountered, and still encounters, foolishness fed by pride.

Three Crucial Virtues

The three cardinal virtues in the kingdom of God are *faith*, *hope*, and *love*. We've already spoken of the centrality of faith in seeing, entering, and experiencing the kingdom; but it is also interwoven with the virtues of hope and love. Paul the apostle more than once put them together in describing the Christian life and ministry: "But now abide faith, hope, love, these three; but the greatest of these is love."[13]

Faith is essential to the functioning of a civilization. We daily reveal faith in the laws of the creation. How could the world function if it didn't have faith that there would be a tomorrow? How could medical doctors and scientists function without faith in an orderly universe? How could we exist without faith, to some degree, in other people? How could we conduct business

---

[13] 1 Corinthians 13:13.

without faith in the marketplace and the rules of commerce? Nothing would work without some kind of faith.

Since we as spiritual beings are saved by the grace of God "through faith,"[14] it is obvious that faith is indispensable in any relationship with the Lord. Without it, we don't even know God exists. We are lost in our sins and are unable to see or to enter the invisible world, let alone transfer its blessings into this visible one.

As for hope, we need to make a distinction between it and faith. Hope is the ability to transfer our reliance from ourselves to God. It is founded on the sovereignty of God, His total independence of circumstances, His limitlessness.

It does not develop in us until our faith is tried, until under pressure we realize there is a Creator who will work things out for those with whom He is pleased. The apostle Paul described the progression:

Therefore having been justified by faith, we have peace with God through our Lord Jesus Christ, through whom also we have obtained our introduction by faith into this grace in which we stand; and we exult in *hope* of the glory of God. And not only this, but we also exult in our tribulations, knowing that tribulation brings about perseverance; and perseverance, proven character; and proven character, *hope*.[15]

God's purpose is that our faith be tested, expressly to refine and strengthen it. Our endurance purifies and toughens our character; resolute hope in God and His plan results.

Note how Paul concludes the development of his thought: ". . . and hope does not disappoint."[16]

Why is this true? Because hope shaped on the anvil rests in

---

[14]Ephesians 2:8.
[15]Romans 5:1–4.
[16]Romans 5:5.

Him and in the moral rightness of His ultimate purpose—that the wicked will fall and the righteous will be rewarded.[17] Any expectation of the transfer of the blessings of the kingdom into our lives depends on it.

Finally, there must be love, which Paul described as the greatest of the trinity of virtues. Interestingly, it grows out of the other two. Hope grows out of faith, and love grows out of hope.

When a person has hope, when he knows that his future is assured, he stops struggling to maintain his own sphere of dominance; he stops fighting other people. He is willing to let the moral law of God work to defend his place. Then he is free to have concern for the well-being of others. He is no longer threatened and can give himself, his possessions, his life to someone else and know that God will make it right.

This process—and it usually is that rather than an immediate change—was radical in my life. Stepping from the role of aggressive, competitive young lawyer who was just beginning the climb up the power ladder in a major international corporation, to the role of a man whose hope was secured by Almighty God completely altered my life and lifestyle. That hope released my ability to love—to love *real* people in *concrete* ways, not merely abstractly. Those in corporate halls were no longer shallow faces; folks in the hard, dirty streets of New York City were no longer the masses. They were people. I had been set free to express my concern for them, which eventually led my family and me to share our lives—our food, our clothing, our shelter—with others in one of the most wretched sections of New York. Our concern took on visible expression.

The Lord's experience with the cross was the ultimate expression of hope and love, of course. He had no visible assurance that He wouldn't be found absolutely foolish. He could have turned out to have been the most tragic figure in history, but He had

---

[17]See Psalm 37:9.

hope in the rightness and goodness of His Father. He was free to love His people and to die for them.

Hope and love are what we must have, Paul said, if we are to experience the power of God in the world today. Love is the strongest force possible. The reason is simple: God *is* love. No negative can overcome that positive. The perpetrators of hate and darkness have tried since the beginning, but the light from Him has prevailed.[18]

Love is so overwhelming that it nullifies the physical principle under which every action produces an opposite, equal reaction. If someone pushes someone else, the latter will push hard in return, and escalation develops, usually to the point of violence. But Jesus said, "Absorb the push. Break the cycle. Overcome evil with good."[19]

We need to see that He wasn't advocating merely defense, but rather the perfect offense with the only weapon capable of absorbing and defeating evil. If someone demands you to go one mile, you can fight him; you can go sullenly and curse him all the way, feeling beaten and rejected. Or you can go on the attack and follow the charter of the kingdom: " 'And whoever shall force you to go one mile, go with him two.' "[20] Love will thus heap burning coals on his head, and the conviction of the Lord will work in His life for good.[21]

Yes, any of us who yearn to see our world changed and have been disappointed by the relative impotence of the people of God must examine ourselves regarding the virtue of love. For the picture painted by Paul in one of his most famous discourses has to convince us that, were love to underlie all of our thoughts, words, and deeds—our use of the principles of God—then the world *would* be changed.

---

[18]See John 1:5.
[19]See Romans 12:21.
[20]Matthew 5:41.
[21]See Romans 12:20.

Love is patient, love is kind, and is not jealous; love does not brag and is not arrogant, does not act unbecomingly; it does not seek its own, is not provoked, does not take into account a wrong suffered, does not rejoice in unrighteousness, but rejoices with the truth; bears all things, believes all things, hopes all things, endures all things. Love never fails . . .[22]

Eventually, Paul said, all else will pass away. The special gifts and talents, the wonderful endowments from on high—they will all run their course. But love endures forever, bridging eternity.

Holy Paradoxes

I trust it is abundantly clear that the constitution of the kingdom of God (the priorities of anyone who would experience the power and blessings of life there) is riddled with paradox. One can almost hear the Lord chuckle as the world looks in disbelief at what would appear to be anti-principles, in light of the way most people and nations conduct their affairs.

The world says hate your enemies. The kingdom says love your enemies.

The world says hit back. The kingdom says do good to those who mistreat you.

The world says hold onto your life at any cost. The kingdom says lose your life and you will find it.

The world says a young and beautiful body is essential. The kingdom says even a grain of wheat must die if it is to have life.

The world says push yourself to the top. The kingdom says serve if you want to lead.

The world says you are number one. The kingdom says many who are first will be last and the last first.

The world says acquire gold and silver. The kingdom says store up treasure in heaven if you would be rich.

---

[22]1 Corinthians 13:4–8.

The world says exploit the masses. The kingdom says do good to the poor.

Sadly, the church itself has often been a leader among those blinded to the paradoxes of the kingdom of God. So many times congregations have fled from the inner city, where they are so desperately needed, to comfortable suburbs, where they could luxuriate and not have to face the poor and their problems. Or they have served a political or social movement rather than the needy. Or they have embraced the management techniques of corporations rather than the government techniques of God. In short, they lost the sound of truth.

If we live for this world—if we seek to grasp it—then we will die to the kingdom. But if we lose ourselves in love and service for others, then we will find ourselves in the kingdom.

The temptations of worldly thinking are great, but they must be resisted even at the cost of appearing foolish by embracing truths that are paradoxical to conventional wisdom.

You see, one major paradox that we must accept as we try to change the world is this: The people of God are to live out the Beatitudes and the virtues of humility, wisdom, faith, hope, and love while at the same time becoming leaders.

" 'You are the light of the world . . . ,'" Jesus said.[23] In darkness, a light does not follow; it leads.

Yes, the humble, the disciplined, the wise, the faithful, the hopeful, the loving—they are to lead. *That* is a holy paradox.

And how will it be brought to pass? The laws of the kingdom will show us.

---

[23]Matthew 5:14.

PART II
LAWS OF THE KINGDOM

SEVEN

THE LAW OF RECIPROCITY

ஜ்ஜ் One simple declaration by Jesus revealed a law that will change the world: " 'Give, and it will be given to you . . .' "[1]

Eight words. They form a spiritual principle that touches every relationship, every condition of man, whether spiritual or physical. They are pivotal in any hope we have of relieving the world's worsening crises.

Jesus expanded the universality of this theme throughout His ministry, varying subject matter and application. His point was so encompassing that it demanded many illustrations. In the discourse from which we get the eight words, we find this expansion: " '. . . just as you want people to treat you, treat them in the same way.' "[2] And from that, of course, came what the

---

[1]Luke 6:38.
[2]Luke 6:31.

world describes as the Golden Rule: "Do unto others as you would have them do unto you."

Jesus went on, putting a frame around the eight key words in this manner:

"Be merciful, just as your Father is merciful. And do not judge and you will not be judged; and do not condemn, and you will not be condemned; pardon, and you will be pardoned. Give, and it will be given to you; good measure, pressed down, shaken together, running over, they will pour into your lap. For by your standard of measure it will be measured to you in return."[3]

By putting this together with the world's greatest teaching on love, repeated from the Old Testament by Jesus as the heart of God's will, we establish the perfect "law" for conduct: " '. . . You shall love your neighbor as yourself.' "[4]

A Universal Principle

The Law of Reciprocity, a kingdom principle revealed in these teachings of the Lord, is relatively easy for us to identify since it is so visibly pervasive in the physical world. As we noted in the previous chapter, a basic law of physics says that for every action there is an equal and opposite reaction. The jet age in which we live is founded on it.

Scientists some years ago must have said, "If we can push a jet of hot air out the back end of an engine, there has to be an equal and opposite reaction going forward. Now, if we can attach this to an airplane, the thrust will be unprecedented."

Of course the logical, parallel step produced rocket engines able to generate enough backward thrust to provide forward

---

[3]Luke 6:36–38.
[4]Matthew 22:39, see also Leviticus 19:18.

speeds necessary to break the hold of gravity and send machines and men into outer space.

In the interpersonal realm, we find the same principle prevailing. If you smile at someone, he most likely will smile back. If you strike someone, the chances are he will hit you back. If you express kindness, you are almost certain to have someone express kindness in return. If you are critical of everything and everyone, you can expect to receive critical judgment from others.

A number of years ago, not long after our family moved to the Tidewater area of Virginia to begin the Christian Broadcasting Network, I remarked to my uncle, a man of admirable maturity, "The people in Tidewater are so very nice, far more so than I had even expected."

My uncle's eyes twinkled and he spoke a powerful, homespun version of the Law of Reciprocity that I hope I never forget: "I tell you what, young man, you will find nice people anywhere you go if you're nice to them."

It is a principle built into the universe. Even international relations respond to it. We Americans saw it at work from the earliest days of the conflict that escalated into the Vietnam War. The escalation was gradual at first. The North Vietnamese and Viet Cong would push at our allies and us. And we would push back, a little harder. They would retaliate, harder, and then back we would come. In such fashion, the United States participated in a dragged-out war that sapped its resources and resolve, simply because of an unwillingness on either side to break the cycle.

This should have been done in one of two ways.

First, we could have loved the enemy and all Southeast Asians, giving them food, clothing, and housing, and doing everything possible to establish them in freedom and the love of God. Love is able to absorb evil actions without fighting back, thus disrupting the cycle of tit for tat. Great faith and courage would have been required while awaiting reciprocal love.

105

Second, we could have hit the enemy so fast and so devastatingly as to nullify reciprocal action. Because of the ultimate infallibility of the Law of Reciprocity, however, it seems almost certain that the latter course would have at a point in history, perhaps distant, produced reciprocity from some source. Recall, for instance, the low estate to which biblical Babylon fell from its days of great, but frequently cruel, empire.

The point, however, is that the Law of Reciprocity functions in international relations—for good or for evil. It is immutable.

The Individual Level

I want to look first at the personal level, for that is where our walk with God must begin. The Christian faith *is* personal, although it quickly spreads to the interpersonal, the national, and the international. It is rarely private for long.

Nonetheless, individuals today are in crisis, and the Law of Reciprocity is important to them.

Jesus, as we have seen, said, "Give, and it shall be given unto you; good measure, pressed down, and shaken together, and running over, shall men give into your bosom. . . ."[5] What words for those today who are suffering economically, threatened with unemployment or foreclosure! They, quite bluntly, need money. The stories are much the same: "What do I do? I'm using everthing I have, and still my bills aren't paid. It seems I've been in debt forever."

As simple as it might look, the Law of Reciprocity is the solution. The world sees such thinking as foolishness, but the Lord says it is wisdom—because it is founded on truth.

As we hear Christ's words, " 'Give, and it will be given to

---

[5]Luke 6:38, KJV.

you ,'"[6] they take us immediately to " 'seek ye first His kingdom
. . . and all these things shall be added to you.' "[7] We saw that
"all these things" comprise what one needs to live.

Giving is foundational. You have to give of yourself. You have
to give of your money. You have to give of your time. And this
foundational truth works in both the invisible and the visible
worlds.

It is not complicated. If you want a higher salary in your job,
you have to give more. Those with good salaries are not people
who sit back and scheme and spend all their time thinking of
ways to promote themselves. The people who are recognized in
an organization are those who work harder, think more creatively,
and act more forcefully in behalf of the enterprise. They give.
They are rewarded.

So many people in our age go for a job with one thought in
mind: "What will I get out of it?" Their only concerns are salary,
fringe benefits, and title. They are takers, not givers. And takers
do not go to the head of the list. The top people are those who
say, "I want to do this to help you. Your company has a product
that I can help make successful. I have a plan that I'm certain will
work." They are givers.

We tend to justify our shortcomings in comparison with these
people by hinting at "lucky breaks" or "knowing the right people." But we're wrong. Invariably, those who give concepts,
extra time, personal concern, and the like are the receivers. They
are giving to an organization—and, indirectly, to individuals in
that organization—and they are bound to benefit.

The hard work and overtime must also be accompanied by a
proper attitude, of course. Those who give meanness or anger or
trouble will get it back. " 'Do not judge lest you be judged,' "[8]

---

[6]Luke 6:38.
[7]Matthew 6:33.
[8]Matthew 7:1.

the Lord said, which drives directly at attitudes. Anyone who is critical, constantly faulting others and cutting associates, will not rise to the top. He will get back what he gives. The one who makes his department look good, including his boss, is the one who will get the salary increase he needs. ". . . By your standard of measure it will be measured to you in return."[9] That's a law.

We cannot talk about a need for money without running headlong into the matter of giving to the Lord. Since everything is His—the cattle on a thousand hills, silver, gold, governments—He obviously is the one we should be turning to in our need. "Give, and it shall be given to you," Jesus said. And that includes our dealing with God Almighty.

The prophet Malachi was precise in speaking the thoughts of the Lord regarding such dealings.

"From the days of your fathers you have turned aside from My statutes, and have not kept them. Return to Me, and I will return to you," says the LORD of hosts. "But you say, 'How shall we return?' Will a man rob God? Yet you are robbing Me! But you say, 'How have we robbed Thee?' *In tithes and offerings.* You are cursed with a curse, for you are robbing Me, the whole nation of you! *Bring the whole tithe* into the storehouse, so that there may be food in My house, and *test Me now in this,*" says the LORD of hosts, "*if I will not open for you the windows of heaven, and pour out for you a blessing until it overflows.*"[10]

The passage shows how seriously the Lord God takes the matter of giving. Obviously, if He owns everything, He doesn't really need our tithes and offerings, but He has gone to great lengths to teach us how things work. If we want to release the superabundance of the kingdom of heaven, we must first give. Our Father is more than ready to fulfill His side of the Law of Reciprocity. One can almost imagine His heavenly host standing

---

[9]Luke 6:38.
[10]Malachi 3:7–10.

on tiptoe, brimming with anticipation, gleeful, awaiting the opportunity to release the treasures so badly needed in our visible world.

Note the promise of abundance in Malachi's words. Some translators render the promised blessing as so great that "you won't have enough room to take it in."[11] In the world, we measure return in percentages of six or eight or ten, and sometimes fifteen and twenty. In the kingdom, as we noted earlier, the measures are 3000 percent, 6000 percent, and 10,000 percent— thirty, sixty, and a hundredfold.

That is a beautiful promise for those facing economic distress today. "Test me," says the Lord. "Prove me."

I am as certain of this as of anything in my life: If you are in financial trouble, the smartest thing you can do is to start giving money away. Give tithes and offerings to the Lord. Give time. Give work. Give love. That sounds crazy. But we have seen how the plan of God is filled with paradox. If you need money, then begin to give away some of whatever you have. Your return, poured into your lap, will be great, pressed down and running over.

A Case in Chile

A missionary to Chile shared some insights into this law of the kingdom sometime ago. As pastor of a group of extremely poor peasants, he did everything he could to minister to their needs. He revealed what he considered to be the full counsel of the Lord, teaching the Bible as the Word of God and leading them into many significant and deep understandings.

But one day the Lord spoke as clearly as if He had been

---

[11]Malachi 3:10, TLB.

standing face to face with him. "You have not declared my whole truth to these people," He said.

"But Lord," the missionary replied. "I don't understand. I've taught them about justification by faith and forgiveness of sins and baptism in the Holy Spirit, about miracles and walking in Your power. I've taught them about the church, about history, about doctrine. I've taught them about godliness and holy living, about the Second Coming.

"What, my Lord, have I failed to teach them?"

He waited a moment. The voice was very clear. "You have not declared my tithe to them."

The missionary was stunned. "But Lord, these are very poor people! They hardly have enough to live. I can't ask them to tithe. They have nothing."

Again, a silent moment. "You must declare to them my tithe."

He was a faithful, obedient man. And the debate ended.

The next Sunday morning, with heavy heart, he stepped into the pulpit of the little rustic church in that poor, backward community, took a deep breath, and began.

"My beloved brethren," he said, looking into the open, up-lifted faces of his flock, "God has shown me that I haven't been faithful in declaring to you His whole counsel. There is something you have not been doing that I must tell you about. You have not been tithing to the Lord."

And he began a trek through the Scriptures with them that lasted nearly an hour. He explained everything, including the Malachi portions urging that the Lord be proven on the matter.

The next Sunday, it was their turn. In they came, obedient to the Word. They didn't have money, so they brought eggs, chickens, leather goods, woven articles, and all manner of things from their poor peasant homes. The altar area was heaped high.

The missionary felt badly about taking the gifts, but he too was faithful, so he sold some and used the money for the work of the church. He distributed some of the gifts to the destitute in the neighborhood and kept some for his own sustenance, in lieu of income.

The same thing happened Sunday after Sunday. The people tithed.

It wasn't long before the effects of drought were seen throughout the countryside. Poverty gripped the people of the land worse than ever. Crops failed; buildings deteriorated; gloom covered everything.

But, miraculously, this was not so with the members of that little church. Their crops flourished as though supernaturally watered. But more than that, the yields were extraordinary, bounteous, healthy, flavorful. Their fields were green, while those around were withering. Their livestock were sleek and strong. Relative abundance replaced abject poverty.

They even had an overflow of crops and goods that could be sold, and before long their tithes included money. They were able to build a much-needed new meeting house.

Despite his misgivings, the missionary and his people had learned that no matter how desperate the situation, no matter how deep the impoverishment, the principles of the kingdom can turn deprivation into abundance.

They touch the visible world.

What Is a Tithe?

Lest we become rigid and legalistic, we need to understand the tithe quantitatively. The word, of course, means a "tenth." People quibble over such questions as whether it is before or after taxes, whether it should go to a single ministry, whether it should be put ahead of absolute necessities, and the like. Such niggling misses the point.

The Lord cherishes a ready giver whose heart puts Him and His service ahead of everything. St. Paul had a lot to declare on this point:

111

Now this I say, he who sows sparingly shall also reap sparingly; and he who sows bountifully shall also reap bountifully. Let each one do just as he has purposed in his heart; not grudgingly or under compulsion; for God loves a cheerful giver. And God is able to make all grace abound to you, that always having all sufficiency in everything, you may have an abundance for every good deed. . . . you will be enriched in everything for all liberality. . . .[12]

According to the dictionary, the original definition of tithe was one-tenth of the annual produce of one's land or of one's annual income. According to the Bible, that is merely the *starting place* of giving to the Lord. The Malachi passage refers to "tithes and offerings." One might say, then, that there is no offering until the tithe has been paid; it is the expected, minimum amount.

So a lot of people who practice this critical spiritual law give far more than ten percent of their income to the Lord's work. It's all His anyhow, they recognize. King David voiced this when he said:

"Both riches and honor come from Thee, and Thou dost rule over all. . . . But who am I and who are my people that we should be able to offer as generously as this? For all things come from Thee, and from Thy hand we have given Thee."[13]

He also wrote in one of his great psalms:

The earth is the LORD's, and the fulness thereof; the world, and they that dwell therein.[14]

Therefore, many people ignore any ten percent cutoff and give out of the abundance of their provision. I know one New Jersey florist who had been thoroughly blessed by the Lord as he exercised the principles we are exploring in this book, and he

---

[12]2 Corinthians 9:6–8,11.
[13]1 Chronicles 29:12,14.
[14]Psalm 24:1, KJV.

frequently gave ninety percent of his annual income to the service of God. And the prosperity simply mounted. He was not able to outgive the Lord. That law is built into the kingdom. It never changes.

One of the saddest things that can happen to people comes about so naturally. When hard times come, when they are thrown out of work or inflation runs wild, the first place they cut is often their tithe. Usually their intentions are good. "I'll make it up next week," they rationalize. And God lets them go. He does not pressure. But that is the worst thing they can do. That, I believe, is the time to step up your giving. That is the time you need something from God. "Prove me," the Lord says. " 'Give, and it will be given to you . . . .' "15

One of the many men who served the Lord in the rescue missions and other street ministries during the Depression of the thirties has reported very moving accounts about those who would pass through the soup kitchen—broken, smashed men, virtually destroyed—where he would often ask them about their spiritual lives.

"Tell me, friend, were you faithful to the Lord with your tithes?" he would inquire.

And the man would shake his head no, clutching his cup and plate in front of him, staring vacantly ahead.

And he'd ask the next one, "When you were prosperous and all was well with you, did you give to the Lord? Were you faithful with your tithe?"

The man would shake his head no.

Never once, this worker reported, did he find a man living in poverty who had been faithful to the Lord and His principle of giving. And that fits exactly with what David said thousands of years ago: "I have been young, and now I am old; Yet I have

---

15Luke 6:38.

not seen the righteous forsaken, Or his descendants begging bread."[16]

We must not misunderstand any of this to say that should there be a general economic collapse, we will see Christians riding in Rolls-Royces, wearing big jewels and rich furs, and living in mansions while everyone else lives in poverty. That would be contrary to the nature of God. It merely means that, if we have been faithful to the Lord, given to Him, given to the poor, given to our neighbor, then we will receive according to the prosperity of the Lord, not the prosperity of the ungodly.

We will experience the fulfillment of seeking first the kingdom of God and having the things necessary for life given to us additionally, even matter-of-factly, if you will.

Those who ignore God's principles, on the other hand, can be expected in a moment, a flash, to find themselves totally stripped of what they thought was theirs.

Yet a little while and the wicked man will be no more;
And you will look carefully for his place, and he will not be there.
But the humble will inherit the land,
And will delight themselves in abundant prosperity.[17]

The Example of Slavery

As we have noted, the Law of Reciprocity works in all the affairs of men. It can work for our good, or it can work for our harm. Americans saw it fulfilled in racial relationships, with roots going back to the days of slavery.

In one of the horrors of history, our representatives went to Africa, seized human beings, stored them in ships, and brought them here to treat like property. We sold them and put them out as forced labor, mistreating them, breaking up families, and

---

[16]Psalm 37:25.
[17]Psalm 37:10,11.

ignoring their rights and dignity as people created in the image of God.

" 'Give, and it will be given to you. . . .' "

It took a hundred years, but our land has been reaping what it sowed. In many cases, blacks were forced into a matriarchal society as men were totally destroyed emotionally, psychologically, and spiritually. Women struggled to put bread on the table for their children, who soon perceived the cause of their suffering and were ripe for hatred.

Guilt and resentment often overtook the whites. The sides of conflict were locked in. And it came. A good nation was battered, its regions divided, its people torn.

Even though education has been improved, rights defended, and poverty relieved, the suffering continues. The government itself teeters under the threat of bankruptcy as it is unable to meet the demands of sickness, unemployment, welfare, inner-city redevelopment, and other social distress, much of it traceable to the deprivation of the black man centuries ago.

Signs of a possible turnaround through proper use of the Law of Reciprocity, which again identifies slavery as the cause of much that went wrong in America, can be seen in the economic recovery of the South. For many years, the southern economy foundered, hostage to the northern banking and commercial interests, because the region did not have properly trained and educated people capable and desirous of working in factories and offices. Without these wage-earners, there were also few customers for southern manufacturers, and prosperity eluded all.

But once the South began to give freedom to the black people, providing education and taking other steps to lift their standard of living, the economy edged upward and soon reached boom level in many places. The South prospered as it never had.

Quite simply, the society had cursed itself. But the Law of Reciprocity, still lacking in many dimensions of life, had made it possible to reverse the curse.

115

I saw the very opposite of the national racial experience unfold on the streets of Portsmouth, Virginia, one day in 1960, only to be snuffed out, all through the working of the reciprocity principle.

A friend, Dick Simmons, was visiting shortly after my family and I had moved to Tidewater, and he asked if we could go preach on the streets in some of the poor sections of the city. We ended up going to a shopping center in the middle of an area of recent racial violence.

We began by engaging a number of black youths in conversation, and before long several dozen had gathered. Dick preached to them about Jesus. The Holy Spirit moved upon all of us, and after a few minutes, Dick said, "Now if you want to meet Jesus, the one I'm talking about, you can do that right here, right now. You bow your head and kneel right here on the sidewalk and pray, and ask Jesus to come into your life."

What a unique gathering that was! In the middle of one of the city's tensest areas, where violence had already erupted, love and peace and beauty descended. Here were two white men giving love and knowledge and experience—giving the truth of the gospel—to a group of deprived, volatile black youngsters, and what did we get in return? We received love and kindness and warmth back from them.

In an instant, even as the youngsters were praying the sinner's prayer and lives were being changed, everything exploded into a surrealistic movie scene. Two cars of police with trained dogs wheeled to a stop. Men and dogs piled out and charged the kneeling black youngsters. The policemen had jumped to a hasty conclusion, prompted by a phone call from a bystander, that a racial protest was mounting, and they intended to break it up. They chased the youngsters across the street as growls and yells filled the air.

In a twinkling, the Law of Reciprocity set in. The youngsters began to throw rocks at the policemen. Yells turned to curses.

And the violence escalated, with all the potential of the devastation that shattered American cities in the sixties.

Dick and I had given love; we had received love. The police had given harshness; they had received harshness. Unhappily the latter pattern prevailed through most of the land.

Potential for the World

Convinced that the Law of Reciprocity could bring relief, if not total solution, to the major problems of the world, I began shortly after dawn one morning early in the decade to make notes on these problems. In less than an hour I had covered the spectrum: The Law of Reciprocity without question affects the way people and nations live with each other. It has the potential to bring peace to the world.

Following are merely a few of the issues I jotted down, but they are widespread enough to make the case. Remember, under the Law of Reciprocity, men everywhere would operate under the principle of giving what they expect to receive, treating others the way they want to be treated, and loving their neighbors as themselves.

War. The need for standing armies would be removed as nations give as they receive and love their neighbors as themselves. The threat of invasion would be gone. Defense appropriations would be unnecessary. Huge governmental spending and the cruelty of high inflation and high taxes would be relieved.

Trade. There would be no need for tariff barriers because nations and companies would not be dumping products and damaging domestic industries. Trade would occur as needed and desired, fostered by healthy, imaginative competition, uninterrupted by runaway greed. Terms like "Third World" would become meaningless.

Injustice. Incredible extremes of wealth and poverty would be

117

evened out simply by human kindness and generosity. The unjust privileges of wealth and other types of status would diminish, melting away envy, jealousy, greedy ambition, and perverted competitiveness.

Crime. Burglary, theft, and vandalism would vanish, along with personal assaults, murder, rape, and kidnapping. Narcotics usage and traffic would cease. Business and securities fraud would pass, cheating at every level would fade, along with price-fixing, monopoly and cartel abuse, and influence-peddling. International terrorism would end. Prisons would become obsolete.

Pollution. Air, water, and land could be cleaned up. There would be no more factories belching acid smoke into the air and draining chemical waste into rivers. Beer cans, bottles, and garbage would vanish from the roadsides and campsites. Parks would retain their beauty. Wildlife would flourish.

Productivity. As the Japanese have learned from their change of heart after World War II, moving from a people known for cheap merchandise to one prospering from excellence, nations would see their economies improve radically through increased productivity in every sector. Employers and employees alike would see sharp changes in their motivation, satisfaction, and collective prosperity. There would be no more shoddy products, no more dangerous construction in which buildings collapse and hundreds are injured or killed, no more unsafe toys to maim children.

Government. Huge governmental bureaucracy would disappear as overdrawn, rigid regulation and enforcement becomes unnecessary, along with most of the social services. As men begin to treat one another as God intended, the governments could concentrate on those relatively few things that must be done collectively.

Renegades Excluded

Many people rightly ask, "Can this law be made to work in the world today? Can we simply begin to live this way?"

I believe the answer is yes, with an exception.

The Law of Reciprocity when practiced by law-abiding people and nations will not work with a totally lawless renegade. To begin to practice this principle with one such as that is extraordinarily dangerous, and a distinction must be made.

However, if you analyze it, you will see that even this exception is a fulfillment of the reciprocity principle. As the renegade gives (living outside law and decency) so will he receive from the entire society, in force. He will be ostracized. That, in a sense, was God's answer to the problem when He called forth His people Israel. They were not to temporize. The renegade was removed from society and rendered incapable of such conduct through very harsh punishment.[18]

For us, the example is found in the New Testament. Jesus did not turn the other cheek to the devil or anyone governed by the devil throughout His ministry. Instead, He exercised His authority. As James said: ". . . Resist the devil and he will flee from you."[19] Oppose him and those belonging to him. They are renegades.

It should be noted that the need to act quickly against the renegade in our society explains why the Law of Reciprocity does not encompass pacifism. For domestic tranquility, there must be a police force and a system of justice capable of bringing sure and swift punishment upon those who rebel against society. Injustice in the administration of the law will bring on revolution. But lack of diligence in the punishment of crime will promote anarchy.

So also in the international realm, the family of peace-loving

---

[18]E.g., Exodus 21,22; Leviticus 18:24, 20:1–27, 21:9.
[19]James 4:7.

nations must be able to protect itself against renegades. The Law of Reciprocity would forbid two equals from beginning a fight to settle a dispute. However, a miscreant is not the equal of law-abiding persons. A rogue nation is not the equal of the family of nations. A rebellious child is not the equal of his parents. In each of these cases, the lawful and just application of discipline or restraint does not violate the Law of Reciprocity. Such discipline is in fact a God-given, albeit temporary, method of dealing with evil in a still imperfect world.

But in all other cases, I believe we should exercise the Law of Reciprocity to the fullest, even among those not yet committed personally to God Almighty. For it is a principle that will work in the visible world—now.

EIGHT

THE LAW OF USE

᪣ An exceptional urgency seemed to have gripped the Lord's ministry by the time He reached the teaching we will examine at this point. He had so much to impart and seemingly so little time to do it. Everything was speeding up.

In the midst of rapid-fire teachings about the kingdom of heaven, He began this story:

"For it is just like a man about to go on a journey, who called his own slaves, and entrusted his possessions to them. And to one he gave five talents, to another, two, and to another, one, each according to his own ability; and he went on his journey."[1]

Then unfolds the development of what I have come to call the Law of Use. Servant number one received five talents. The parable says he went out and " 'traded with them.' " We can

---

[1]Matthew 25:14,15ff.

imagine what happened. Perhaps he bought some commodities, sold them at a profit, and reinvested the entire amount. Or perhaps he took a journey and returned with valuable goods, and he added to the value of those goods through work he or someone else did to them. Regardless, he worked with his master's money and eventually doubled it.

The man with the two talents acted similarly. He may have bought wool, handed it over to a weaver, and then sold the woven cloth at a profit, only to quickly reinvest it and keep all the money working. Eventually he had doubled the amount left with him.

The third slave acted differently, however. The parable says he took the single talent, dug a hole, and buried it. He was afraid, Jesus said—afraid that if he went out and bought wool or oil or some such item, a depression would come and he would lose the money. Or maybe robbers would steal it. Or maybe someone would outsmart him or cheat him, say, at the weights and balances. Perhaps he would make a wrong decision. So, impotent with fear, he preserved his lord's investment by hiding it in a safe place.

After a long time, the lord returned and called the slaves to him. "Tell me," he said after a brief exchange, "how did you do with my money?"

The first servant quickly replied, "Master, I took the five talents and I traded with them. I bought and sold, and even wheeled and dealed a little bit, and I made five more talents. Here is the original and five additional."

He had covered his overhead and still doubled the amount.

The master was pleased: " '. . . Well done, good and faithful slave; you were faithful with a few things. I will put you in charge of many things; enter into the joy of your master.' "

The next servant stepped forward and reported: "Lord, I took your two talents, and I went out and bought and sold. I entered into some business transactions, and I took some risks, but I made money. I've got two more talents. Here are the two you gave me and two additional."

The lord replied in the same way he had to the man with five talents.

Then it was the third man's turn. "Tell me what you've done with my money while I've been gone," the master said.

"Lord, I knew you were a hard man," he began. "You reap where you don't sow. You gather where you don't even plant. So I was afraid. I figured the best thing to do was play it safe, so I wrapped the talent up nicely and hid it. Here it is; I didn't lose anything."

Most of us today can sympathize with this fellow. After all, if you're a trustee over somebody else's property, you have to be careful. You can't take risks. It's even worse in an economically volatile world like ours.

What did the master do in this illustration to prepare us for the kingdom?

". . . 'You wicked, lazy slave, you knew that I reap where I did not sow, and gather where I scattered no seed. Then you ought to have put my money in the bank, and on my arrival I would have received my money back with interest. . . . cast out the worthless slave into the outer darkness; in that place there shall be weeping and gnashing of teeth."[2]

The man was considered wicked—sinful, given to evil—because he refused to take what his lord had given him and put it to work, improving upon it.

Note that quantity wasn't the key. Their use of what they had been given was what mattered. Proper use gave them entry into the place of joy. Improper use barred the third man.

However, the startling point of the parable is the following conclusion: ". . . 'to everyone who has shall more be given, and

---

[2]Matthew 25:26,27,30.

he shall have an abundance; but from the one who does not have, even what he does have shall be taken away.'"[3] During my extended time of seeking wisdom from God, the magnitude of that sentence crystallized for me. I perceived that it presented a principle, a law, that was as important for day-to-day life as any there is.

" 'To everyone who has shall more be given.' " It seems shocking, particularly to those tending toward a welfare state or socialism, as so many in the world do today. We have a poor man with only one talent and another who has improved his lot, and we take the one away from the former and give it to the one who already has ten. It goes against the grain, simply because we have failed to see how important God views our use of what He has given us.

Despite our preconceived attitudes toward social justice, God's Law of Use controls the ultimate distribution of wealth. We must be willing to take the world as He made it and live in it to the fullest. For He says, in fact, that if we are willing to do that—if we are willing to use what He has given us—we will have more. But if we are not willing to use what He has given us, we will lose it.

As we will see, this is not mean or unfair. It is the way *God* wants the world to be. And as we begin to understand the Law of Use, we will soon realize that this is the only way it can be.

Muscles Respond, Too

Our bodies give us a perfect illustration of the working of the Law of Use. For instance, let's say you would like to learn to do push-ups. Perhaps you've never been able to do them well.

---

[3]Matthew 25:29.

I will assume the Lord has given you the strength to do one, perhaps only the kind from the knees, called a woman's pushup; but you can do that. And so you take what you have, and you put it to work. Do one a day for a week or two and before long you'll find it's not hard. Then go to two, and do two for a week or two. They'll get easier, and then you can move to three, and so on. Before long you'll be doing ten, and you'll start to wonder, "Why did I think these were so hard?"

Do you see the simple principle? To everyone who has, and who uses what he has, more shall be given.

Now, you could do the very opposite. You could take what you have, refuse to use it, and ultimately lose it. For instance, you could tape your hand to your side in such a way that you would be unable to move it. If you left it there, totally unused, for six months, the muscles would wither and an arm that had had unlimited potential would be useless. Even what you had would have been taken away.

The same would hold true for the development of your mind and resultant skills. If you were a doctor, say, and wanted to master a particular type of treatment, you would begin simply with the knowledge you had. You could study everything available, and you could practice your knowledge, simply at first, perhaps under close supervision. You could stay at it for a year or two and before long, you would master the subject. You would have expertise and a specialty that others would covet, all acquired through using what you already had.

Of course, if you thoroughly neglected study and abstained totally from practice, you would gradually reach a point of deterioration and incompetence where no one would want to trust himself in your hands. You would lose what you started with.

So also in our spiritual lives. If we pray, read the Bible, and exercise the understanding we already have, we will grow. If we don't, we will weaken and diminish in effectiveness.

125

Carver and the Peanut

One of the geniuses of our country was a black man named George Washington Carver. He perfectly illustrated the Law of Use in a different fashion.

One day he went before the Lord in prayer and said, "Mr. Creator, show me the secrets of Your universe."

It was a big request, but he believed in asking boldly.

He received a bold answer, although it might not have seemed so at first.

"Little man," God said, "you're not big enough to know the secrets of My universe."

One can almost feel the sense of repudiation. However, God was not finished with His reply. "But I'll show you the secret of the peanut."

From the universe to the peanut! "Take it apart," God said.

Undaunted and obedient, Carver did just that. He took the peanut apart and discovered several hundred elements in that little seed.

Still God wasn't finished. "Start putting it back together again, in different form," the Lord instructed.

He did. And from that work came food of many kinds, plastics, paint, oil, and seemingly endless products. He revolutionized Southern agriculture and industry all by using what God had given—boldly, creatively, patiently.

The Exponential Curve

Working hand in hand with the Law of Use is a mathematical phenomenon known as the exponential curve. Actually Jesus set forth the first step in such a curve when He told the parable of the talents. It fits perfectly into our principle.

The Lord told how two of the servants doubled what had been

given to them. Had they done that at regular intervals, such as annually, then their increases, placed on a graph, would have established an exponential curve that would have proved astounding.

For example, if they began with $100 and continued to double the amount each year, the graph would proceed along at a rather ho-hum level for a few years and then it would skyrocket. At the end of twenty years, the $100 would have grown to $50 million. In just five more years, it would have soared to $1.6 billion. By the thirty-five-year mark, it would be $1.6 trillion, and at the end of fifty years, it would be $12.8 quadrillion, which is more money than exists in the world.

This shows dramatically what can happen through a joining of the Law of Use with the exponential curve, simply accomplishing at a set rate what Jesus was teaching in the parable.

Of course, such 100 percent increases are not necessary for the exponential curve to be effective with this law. Take the $100 and compound it at six percent for fifty years and it is transformed into nearly $2,800. Increase the percentage to 15 or 20 percent and you end up with several hundred thousand dollars.

So phenomenal is this principle that Baron Rothschild, the financier, once described compound interest as "the eighth wonder of the world." Bankers throughout history have enriched themselves enormously by way of this "wonder." The key is consistency and longevity, to the point where the exponential curve makes its sharp upward turn, and the escalation defies the imagination.

Certainly, the Lord Jesus did not intend to lay down for us a principle whose purpose was to allow the rich to get richer and the poor to get poorer. No, He was showing how the world works and how, through diligent, patient exercise of the gifts He is constantly bestowing, we can enter into the prosperity and abundance of the invisible world.

We need to see that the truths He disclosed are available to everyone—now. The sad fact is that not everyone—not even those committed to Him—will enter in. We are too much like the servant who took his talent and buried it.

The problem often is that we will look at someone successful in a field we would like to be in and say, "I wish I were like him." We want to have the success without having applied the Law of Use and the exponential curve. We want to go from obscurity and poverty to fame and riches in one quick jump. First we have to take what He has given and multiply it, steadily and patiently. Success will come.

To want full accomplishment immediately is lust. It is a sin and calls for violation of the pattern of God. It is wanting something for nothing. Socialism and communism feed on such lust, calling for taking from the rich and giving to the poor, for leveling society in such a way as to deprive individuals of the learning and maturity necessary to handle abundance.

So many well-meaning people have in fact done harm to individuals and indeed to nations by short-cutting God's plan and short-circuiting the blessings intended. They want to give everyone everything immediately, not only stirring up lust, but also fulfilling it, and ultimately harming those they want to help.

God's way is the way of gradual, sure growth and maturity, moving toward perfection. It can be compared to an airplane during takeoff. If the trajectory is too low, then time will overtake it, the plane will run out of runway and crash, or it will get a few feet off the ground and not rise fast enough to avoid the trees or buildings.

People are the same. If their goals are too low, too stretched out and easy, they will never rise to any significant potential before time overtakes them.

On the other hand, if the pilot sets the exponent in his takeoff pattern too high and the plane rises too steeply, it is likely to stall and crash.

The same is true with people. Set your economic growth too

high, and you will stall; try to make your child learn too much too fast, and he will become discouraged and give up; try to do fifty push-ups without practice, and you will encounter agony.

Thus, although there is nothing but abundance in the kingdom of heaven and nothing is impossible with God, the Lord's plan is for us to set realistic goals with what He has given us. He wants us to have goals that are demanding enough to keep us occupied, but are not overtaxing, and to stick with them long enough for them to come to fruition.

We find clues to this in other parables of the Lord.

". . . The kingdom of heaven is like a mustard seed, which a man took and sowed in his field; and this is smaller than all other seeds; but when it is full grown, it is larger than the garden plants, and becomes a tree, so that the birds of the air come and nest in its branches."[4]

The black mustard of the East starts with the tiniest seed imaginable, but from that tiny beginning comes a strong plant often running to heights as tall as a man on horseback. So it can be with the things given to us to use.

Similarly Jesus told of what might be called *unconscious* growth from small beginnings:

And He was saying, "The kingdom of God is like a man who casts seed upon the soil; and goes to bed at night and gets up by day, and the seed sprouts up and grows—how, he himself does not know. The soil produces crops by itself; first the blade, then the head, then the mature grain in the head. But when the crop permits, he immediately puts in the sickle, because the harvest has come."[5]

We must never despise small beginnings. The increase will come, almost unconsciously, imperceptibly, in the early stages;

---

[4]Matthew 13:31,32.
[5]Mark 4:26–29.

but suddenly there will be a burst of growth as the exponential rate takes hold and reaches maturity. Before long, it's harvest time.

Remember, everyone has something. With some, it's music. With some, it's athletics. With some, it's technical skill. Even a quadriplegic confined to bed cannot feel left out of this marvelous principle. Perhaps more important than anything else, he can consistently exercise the great gift of prayer, maturing to remarkable depths and affecting the entire world.

Wrong Side of the Curve

One of the tragedies of man is that he frequently gets himself on the wrong side of the exponential curve; it can work against us as well as for us. This happens to individuals and it happens to nations.

The United States and many of its citizens are examples at this very time. Singly and collectively we have allowed the exponential curve to plunge us into enormous debt. In most cases, the beginnings were innocent, but the exponential rate is merciless if it's working against you. It can destroy you if you are borrowing money and paying high interest rates. Vast numbers of Americans are caught in such traps right now, and our government has been suffering under an increasingly impossible burden for years.

This, of course, comes from the lust and covetousness I mentioned, the insistence on having everything now. "I want my furniture *now*," the housewife cries. Meanwhile her husband demands his new, bigger car—now. Neither wants to await the accumulation of the resources necesssary to avoid sending compound interest careening into action. On a wider scale, our national attitude views many luxuries as necessities. We override the Law of Use when we attempt to put the biggest, most modern television sets and gadgetry in every home and apartment through consumer debt or even through welfare laws. The national debt soars, credit card bills reach astronomical heights, and the exponential curve zooms upward to hopelessness and collapse.

Jesus Himself, coming in the flesh as man and suffering temptation just as we do, ran into a test on this score early in His public ministry. It came during His temptation in the wilderness: "Again, the devil took Him to a very high mountain, and showed Him all the kingdoms of the world, and their glory; and he said to Him, 'All these things will I give You, if You fall down and worship me.' "[6]

Satan, described in the New Testament as " 'the ruler of the world' " (although destined to be cast out),[7] promised Him everything, right then, if He would just do it his way. But the Lord said He would do it God's way—gradually, the way of sacrifice and suffering, the way of work, the way of the cross.

The law of Satan's kingdom is: Have it now, with a splash. Quick money, quick things, quick success.

In God's kingdom, the Law of Use governs, providing genuine and lasting security, genuine and lasting prosperity.

Because of the power of the Law of Use and the exponential curve—along with man's seemingly incurable weaknesses—God many centuries ago established two rules for the people of Israel of which we should be aware.

First, he decreed that the Israelites were not to take usury of one another: " 'You shall not charge interest to your countrymen: interest on money, food, or anything that may be loaned at interest.' "[8]

They were permitted to charge interest to foreigners, which

6Matthew 4:8,9.
7John 12:31,14:30.
8Deuteronomy 23:19.

would agree with the parable of the talents in the New Testament, apparently because the Lord intended to give them dominance over other nations: " 'For the LORD your God shall bless you as He has promised you, and *you will lend to many nations,* but you will not borrow; and *you will rule over many nations,* but they will not rule over you.' "9

Modern experience has shown that usury ultimately leads to subservience; and God did not want that for His people, but rather intended for them to rule.

Second, God set up a year of jubilee for his people to counteract the fact that a few eventually gain control of all wealth and land. In short, He directed that every fifty years all debt be canceled, all accumulated property be redistributed, and the cycle of use begin again.

It was part of His marvelous plan under which the land would have a sabbath year to the Lord. For six years, the land would be worked, " 'but during the seventh year the land shall have a sabbath rest, a sabbath to the LORD.' "10 Then He laid out the jubilee plan:

'You are also to count off seven sabbaths of years for yourself, seven times seven years, so that you have the time of the seven sabbaths of years, namely, forty-nine years. You shall then sound a ram's horn abroad on the tenth day of the seventh month; on the day of atonement you shall sound a horn all through your land. You shall thus consecrate the fiftieth year and *proclaim a release* through the land to all its inhabitants. It shall be a jubilee for you, and each of you shall return to his family.'11

The "release" or "liberty" was multifaceted and touched much of the life of the Israelites, specifically remitting indebtedness. It

---

9Deuteronomy 15:6.
10Leviticus 25:4.
11Leviticus 25:8–10.

was as though God said to a man who perhaps was twenty at the beginning of the cycle and who is now seventy: "You've had your day in the sun, your time of opportunity, so now you should step aside, cancel the debts, and let people start over again."

I believe it is quite possible the year of jubilee will be the only way out, short of collapse for our world in its current economic slide. The United States Government, and indeed all governments, have gotten on the wrong side of the exponential curve and the Law of Use and have reached the point of insupportable debt. Trying to meet the demands of the people who are screaming "We want it now!" the governments, along with individuals, have run at major deficits, borrowing huge sums of money, always at compound interest. Early in the decade, the estimated worldwide debt was $10 trillion, with interest payments reaching the point where nations cannot meet them. The United States itself owed $1 trillion, and efforts to correct its economic trends set off dangerous convulsions.

Notwithstanding the sneers of many in the banking community, it may be that God's way will be the only one open to us—a year of jubilee to straighten out the mess.

We should also be fully aware of the fact that finance is not the only area in which the exponential curve can work against us. We need only look at the snowballing evils of pornography, adultery, divorce, alcoholism, and drug addiction to grasp this. Such evil began small and steadily increased, almost unconsciously it seems, until the unprecedented surge of recent years and today's raging floodtide.

The Most Powerful Principle

In the previous chapter, I said the Law of Reciprocity was probably the most encompassing of the kingdom principles, virtually undergirding every aspect of life and revealing a course of conduct that could change the world.

The Law of Use, meanwhile, coupled with the exponential curve is probably the most powerful of the principles in terms of day-to-day life. It is the fundamental law for the growth and development—or the decline—of all organizations and societies in both the invisible and the visible worlds. Beginning with the cradle, it touches everything—child development, intellectual development, professional development, physical development, social development, and on and on.

Together the Law of Reciprocity and the Law of Use are the core of the way the world works, the invisible world and the visible one.

We have already explored major areas touched by the Law of Use and the exponential curve, but we need to see the never-ending, ever-increasing potential. There is, in fact, a principle of increasing opportunity. For example, the man with $100 has certain vistas of opportunity before him. By applying the Law of Use, he can increase that sum to $1000, and immediately his opportunities for expanded use of the law are increased. Quite simply, the man with $1000 has more clout than the man with $100.

If he presses on with the Law of Use, he will rise to the $10,000 level and his vistas widen; then $100,000 and he finds bank doors and credit open to him that he hadn't dreamed of. A million dollars opens an entirely new class of opportunity, and so it goes—never-ending opportunity for the person involved in the Law of Use.

The broadcasting world works the same way. To him who is faithful in a little will more be given. A person who has worked his way up to ownership of five stations has a far easier time acquiring a sixth than the person just starting out has in acquiring the first. The former is experienced and knowledgeable. He knows when and how to move. He has access to money markets that the inexperienced, struggling beginner lacks.

So it is with people in science. The one who has mastered fundamental and intermediate theorems is far more capable of going on to an advanced theorem than is the youngster who hasn't had his first high school science course.

In politics, the person who has successfully run for a city council seat is more likely to succeed in a race for mayor than someone who is unknown and untested. The mayor is then in a stronger position to move to the state legislature than the beginner, and on up the line to governor, senator, and perhaps president.

The same holds true for spiritual life. The opportunities steadily increase as we move from one level of understanding and maturity to the next. Mastery of one small principle of the faith opens up new horizons for even wider growth. Prayer and intercession for our families builds us up for prayer and intercession for our church, and then our town, our state, and our nation. Similarly, public ministry to fifty people will open opportunities for ministry to one hundred. We are then far better prepared to minister to one thousand, then ten thousand, then twenty thousand.

No, we are not to despise small beginnings, but rather to exercise the eternally established Law of Use.

I am convinced that this law—put to work with the commitment, the virtues, and the accompanying subprinciples—can produce giant steps toward easing and ultimately removing the crises that grip the world. It will touch world hunger, the economic quagmire, energy depletion, Third World needs, educational and social injustice, church evangelism, moral decadence, disease, and inadequate health care.

The only thing lacking is for us to hear with understanding the words spoken by God to Moses regarding the sanctuary Israel

135

was to construct for the Lord: " 'According to all that I am going to show you, as the *pattern* of the tabernacle and the *pattern* of all its furniture, *just so you shall construct it.*' "[12]

"Do it my way," says the Lord. He has given a pattern for the secret kingdom. We merely need to follow it.

---

[12]Exodus 25:9.

NINE

THE LAW OF PERSEVERANCE

We've caught glimpses of it in previous chapters, but we need to see clearly that the ways of the universe yield to perseverance.

We see it in the simple, homely story of the chick and the egg. The baby chick, approaching full life, finds himself in a nice, safe environment, dark and quiet. His home, the egg, keeps him warm and cuddly; he feels just perfect.

Soon, however, he becomes aware that the shell keeping him so comfortable and safe is also circumscribing his life. He begins to feel restricted.

You see, there is something in life that says, "I have to grow." Humans and animals have planted within them the need to be free and to grow.

So the little chick begins pecking at the shell. He doesn't understand it, but things have been set up so that he has to peck and peck and peck. He works very hard, gaining strength hour by hour from that God-ordained struggle. Before long, he has attained the strength and the endurance to cope with a new environment, and he breaks through the shell. He pecks some more, and soon he is free, ready for a new level of life.

People have tried to help little chicks speed the process by cracking the shell and opening it for them. But, short-circuiting God's process, they kill the chicks. They are stillborn, unable to handle for even a few moments the rigors of a new environment.

God's principle is what I call the Law of Perseverance. It is critical to success in life generally and to life in the kingdom especially.

Certain risks go with new life and growth—the risks of freedom, we might say—but God prepares us for those risks, through perseverance and struggle, building our muscles, as it were, for each new phase. To refuse to struggle is to stand still, to stagnate.

Jesus taught the Law of Perseverance in a passage well-known to most Christians:

"Ask, and it shall be given to you; seek, and you shall find; knock, and it shall be opened to you. For everyone who asks receives, and he who seeks finds, and to him who knocks it shall be opened. Or what man is there among you, when his son shall ask him for a loaf, will give him a stone? Or if he shall ask for a fish, he will not give him a snake, will he? If you then, being evil, know how to give good gifts to your children, how much more shall your Father who is in heaven give what is good to those who ask Him!"[1]

We grasp His meaning more fully when we understand that the verbs "asks," "seeks," and "knocks" were written in the Greek present imperative and are to be understood in this manner: "*Keep asking*, and it shall be given to you; *keep seeking*, and you

---

[1]Matthew 7:7–11.

shall find; *keep knocking,* and it shall be opened to you." The Father gives "what is good to those who *keep asking* Him."

He also said, as we have noted, that " '. . . the kingdom of heaven suffers violence, and violent men take it by force.' "[2] It does not come easily. The little chick we spoke of was violent; he had to be. Most of the secrets of God come forth with effort; the blessings of God are the same.

Some Christians have been taught that all one has to do to get things from God is to speak the word of faith, believe, and receive. That comes close to the truth, but it neglects the universal Law of Perseverance. God slowly yields the good things of the kingdom and the world to those who struggle. Jacob, for instance, wrestled all night with an angel before he became Israel, a prince with God. Abraham waited one hundred years before he received Isaac, the child of promise. The people of Judah waited and struggled seventy years in captivity before God brought them home.

This does not negate the necessity for asking in faith, the believing, and the receiving. But many times those steps are only the beginning of the process. The fulfillment may take years.

Jesus gave this illustration of perseverance:

Now He was telling them a parable to show that at all times they ought to pray and not to lose heart, saying, "There was in a certain city a judge who did not fear God, and did not respect man. And there was a widow in that city, and she kept coming to him, saying, 'Give me legal protection from my opponent.' And for a while he was unwilling; but afterward he said to himself, 'Even though I do not fear God nor respect man, yet because this widow bothers me, I will give her legal protection, lest by continually coming she wear me out.' " And the Lord said, "Hear what the unrighteous judge said; now shall not God bring about justice for His elect, who cry to Him day and night, and will He delay long over them? I tell you that He

---

[2]Matthew 11:12.

will bring about justice for them speedily. However, when the Son of Man comes, will He find faith on the earth?"[3]

Jesus knew men inside out. He knew our tendency to give up quickly, to become inconsistent and lackadaisical. Yet He pleaded with us to persist, in prayer and in all aspects of life.

And He said to them, "Suppose one of you shall have a friend, and shall go to him at midnight, and say to him, 'Friend, lend me three loaves; for a friend of mine has come to me from a journey, and I have nothing to set before him'; and from inside he shall answer and say, 'Do not bother me; the door has already been shut and my children and I are in bed; I cannot get up and give you anything.' I tell you, even though he will not get up and give him anything because he is his friend, yet because of his persistence he will get up and give him as much as he needs."[4]

Keep on asking, He said, keep on seeking, and keep on knocking. Don't be afraid even to make a ruckus. God prefers that to slothfulness and indolence. He wants people who will travail and perhaps stumble a bit, but keep on going forward, just like a toddler who's trying to learn to walk. The child builds muscles and learns. One day he will run.

In the early, trying days of the church, according to the Book of Acts, Paul and Barnabas traveled through Lystra, Iconium, and Antioch "strengthening the souls of the disciples, encouraging them to continue in the faith, and saying, 'Through many tribulations we must enter the kingdom of God.'"[5]

There was to be conflict, they said, using a word that most translators have rendered "tribulation" but which carries the idea of "pressure," especially pressure on the spirit. This pressure, or

---

[3]Luke 18:1–8.
[4]Luke 11:5–8.
[5]Acts 14:22.

tribulation, was understood in New Testament times to build stamina and staying power, leading to fullness of characver.

We are to remember that there is an adversary. He is called Satan. One of his favorite techniques in the unrelenting effort to trip the people of God is to foster discouragement and depression. That is why the Bible says repeatedly that Christians are to be patient, to hold on, to persist.

Satan is continuously pouring into our ears such negatives as these: "You're not accomplishing anything. . . . You're on the wrong course. . . . You don't have the necessary skill and ability. . . . Everyone else has failed so why do you think you'll succeed. . . . Those promises you thought were from God are nothing. . . . You're unworthy. . . ."

So we often grow discouraged and quit. Then the principles of the kingdom cease to function in our lives. And we fail.

The ultimate personal failure, of course, is suicide. It is the number two killer of our nation's youth, next to automobile accidents. So many people have given up in hopelessness, finding their problems overwhelming, the world mess beyond repair, the possibilities of life too dark. And they slip into the horror of taking their lives, which truly are not theirs to take.

Even the great prophet Elijah reached such despair. Having experienced one of his great triumphs, the defeat of the priests of Baal through a powerful miracle of God, he obviously was exhausted mentally, emotionally, and physically. Jezebel was trying to kill him. He fell into gloom.

" 'It is enough . . . ,' " he cried out. " 'O LORD, take my life, for I am not better than my fathers.' "[6]

But God would not let him give up. Neither does He want us to quit.

Instead, we are to be constantly alert against discouragement and depression. We are to be aware of what our enemy is trying

---

[6] 1 Kings 19:4.

to do. We are to reject him and he will flee. God will not let trial and temptation overcome us if we will stand, but rather will make a way of victory for us.[7] He wants us to persevere and will make it possible.

Lessons of History

Had God given us no more insight than the Law of Perseverance together with the Laws of Reciprocity and Use, we would have enough to change the world. We need only think of examples from our own national history.

Consider Abraham Lincoln. He became one of the greatest governmental and moral leaders in American history. But the achievements didn't come until he had passed through many personal failures, including bankruptcies and endless humiliating labors to make ends meet. The struggles, the battles, the wounds—they equipped him for the environment in which he would make his greatest contribution.

Consider Thomas Edison. This greatest of inventors went through hundreds of experiments that were failures before he achieved success with the electric light. He attributed his incredible accomplishments to "two percent inspiration and ninety-eight percent perspiration"—a formula for struggle and perseverance.

Consider the Wright Brothers. On the lonely sands of North Carolina's outer banks, they battled the elements, the ridicule of men, the lack of resources. They built; they failed; they rebuilt and failed again. Finally, they flew. And the world was changed.

In my own life's work, through the grace of God, I learned the centrality of perseverance. In 1959 my family and I arrived in Tidewater with $70 and a God-planted desire to establish a

---

[7]See 1 Corinthians 10:13.

broadcasting ministry that would glorify the Lord. We went through two years of personal and corporate struggle before getting on the air with our first station. Then came ten years more of striving, anguish, and hardship before we obtained our second station. Steadily the growth increased, as we persevered and learned the lessons of the kingdom.

In that pressure cooker, which in so many ways resembled the trials of the chick with the egg, we matured to the point of readiness for a worldwide ministry. With hindsight, it is amusing to note how the Lord forced us to use everything He had given us to its very limit before He provided something new. Before establishing us in our new Virginia Beach international center, He had us using every nook and cranny and every foot of property available to us. We had trailers lined up all over the land, jammed with people and activity. We had rented property all over Tidewater, taxing our ingenuity and patience daily. Through it all, we were getting ready for the next phase of our work; we were being strengthened for a new environment and new challenges. We were getting maturity the only way a Christian can get it.

In 1979 I examined CBN's history and found that in those twenty years, the Lord had taken our initial $70 and caused it to double exponentially every year during that time. By sheer mercy and grace, He had led us in the Laws of Reciprocity, Use, and Perseverance.

Had He led us otherwise, dumping on us too quickly the responsibility for a worldwide ministry and budgets of tens of millions of dollars, we would have crumbled. But He is wise enough to lead his people according to His laws even before we are able to know and articulate them.

As the great Bible teacher Donald Gray Barnhouse put it, "God uses oak trees, not mushrooms. " Are not perseverance and strength the great virtues of oak trees?

TEN
THE LAW OF RESPONSIBILITY

Flowing in the same stream with the Laws of Reciprocity, Use, and Perseverance is the Law of Responsibility. Jesus summed it up succinctly: ". . . unto whomsoever much is given, of him shall be much required: and to whom men have committed much, of him they will ask the more."[1]

Using a parable on watchfulness and preparation, He made clear that rejection of this law leads to suffering. Those who are given understanding, ability, goods, money, authority, or fame have a responsibility that the less favored do not bear; failure to fulfill it produces fearful punishment.[2]

Jesus was precise in showing that the parable was for the favored in every category, spiritual and physical, those living in the invisible world and those living in the visible.

---

[1]Luke 12:48, KJV.
[2]See Luke 12:46–48.

Whatever level of opportunity is given to us, both God and man expect us to give a certain standard of performance. Favor carries with it responsibility. As the favor increases, the responsibility increases.

If, for example, I am the steward of $1000 for someone, that person will expect a profit of about $100. But if I'm the steward of General Motors and report a profit of $100, I will be forced to resign in disgrace.

If I'm a tennis player who manages to get on the courts, say, on Saturday afternoons and can hit the ball well enough to get by, my friends will be satisfied. But if I'm given the skill and opportunity to advance to world class and then perform like a weekend player, people will be disappointed and my stature will diminish severely.

Rubinstein, the pianist, capsulized this principle when he remarked that should he fail to practice one day, he would know it; should he skip practice for two days, the critics would know it; but should that extend to three days, "the whole world knows it." A part-time church pianist might get away with a bit of a letdown, but not an internationally acclaimed musician. More is required of the professional.

Exercise of the Law of Use will bring success, especially if done in tandem with the Law of Perseverance, but the rewards of those two laws *demand* observance of the Law of Responsibility. We need to see this even before we expect God to fulfill His promises regarding the other principles. It is very wrong if we ask God for something and then don't accept the responsibility that goes with it.

Harry Truman said it well when remarking on the burden of the presidency: "If you can't stand the heat, get out of the kitchen." The presidency of the United States carries heavy responsibilities, he related; and if one doesn't want to face the responsibilities, he should not seek the favor of the people in the first place. For, as he said at another time, "There is no end to the chain of responsibility that binds [the President], and he is never allowed to forget that he is President." The sign on his Oval Office desk said: "The buck stops here."

At CBN, we have found the burden of favor to be a responsibility never to be forgotten. For example, the Lord blessed us deeply one year, allowing us to lead 75,000 people to acceptance of salvation through Jesus Christ. From that point on, there is no way we or our supporters could be satisfied with leading one thousand people to the Lord, despite the fact that one thousand salvations in one year is an astounding achievement. No, the Lord has given us much—equipment, personnel, opportunity—and much is required, both by God and by man. That's the way it works.

The Church Should Listen

Leaders of the church should be especially careful to rise to the responsibility given to them, for the Scripture is so clear on this point as to be somewhat frightening. I am always stopped momentarily when I read the words of James regarding teachers: "Let not many of you become teachers, my brethren, knowing that as such we shall incur a stricter judgment."[3]

Those who have been shown enough to teach can be expected to practice what they teach, at the very least. The office carries a great responsibility.

Paul's letters to Timothy and Titus show the great expectations of God and man from those desiring to be overseers ("bishops" in the older translations).

It is a trustworthy statement: if any man aspires to the office of overseer [or bishop], it is a fine work he desires to do. An overseer,

---

[3]James 3:1.

then, must be above reproach, the husband of one wife, temperate, prudent, respectable, hospitable, able to teach, not addicted to wine or pugnacious, but gentle, uncontentious, free from the love of money. He must be one who manages his own household well, keeping his children under control with all dignity (but if a man does not know how to manage his own household, how will he take care of the church of God?); and not a new convert, lest he become conceited and fall into the condemnation incurred by the devil. And he must have a good reputation with those outside the church, so that he may not fall into reproach and the snare of the devil.[4]

He goes on to point out that those seeking the lesser office of deacon, while not required to measure up to the full responsibility of overseer or bishop, must nevertheless bear a burden greater than that of most, first being "tested" and found "beyond reproach."[5]

Christ's first disciples, especially the Twelve, carried extraordinary burdens and responsibilities, as the New Testament shows in detail. They had been " 'given the mystery of the kingdom of God' "[6] by the Lord Himself while others heard only in parables. This great gift, in a sense, carried with it the load of the world; and those apostles paid a great price—ridicule, ostracism, persecution, martyrdom—for the opportunity of spreading the gospel. Their sense of responsibility was always before them. In his letter to the Romans, Paul summed up that responsibility with these words: "I am under obligation both to Greeks and to barbarians, both to the wise and to the foolish."[7]

Even the ordinary, little-known people who have received the inexpressibly rich gift of eternal life—by grace through faith—are called to a life far more responsible and demanding than they

---

[4]1 Timothy 3:1–7.
[5]1 Timothy 3:10.
[6]Mark 4:11.
[7]Romans 1:14.

led before. Knowing the Lord, who is " 'the way, the truth, and the life' "[8] sets a standard for us in the sight of God and people that we should always keep in mind. Paul referred to it as knowing how to conduct yourself "in the household of God, which is the church of the living God, the pillar and support of the truth."[9] It is a significant responsibility each Christian must meet. We need only look at the Great Commission given by Jesus to His people just before His ascension.

. . . "All authority has been given to Me in heaven and on earth. Go therefore and make disciples of all the nations, baptizing them in the name of the Father and the Son and the Holy Spirit, teaching them to observe all that I commanded you. . . ."[10]

Even though He had said He Himself would build His church,[11] the responsibility for carrying that plan forward for the entire world was put into the hands of His people. *That* is responsibility.

Rank and Responsibility

Early in the nineteenth century, a French duke, Gaston Pierre Marc, wrote in a collection of *Maxims and Reflections* a two-word statement that has become part of our language: "*Noblesse oblige.*" Despite historical abuses, it expresses the essence of the Law of Responsibility. "Nobility obliges" or, better, "nobility obligates" states the obligation of people of high rank, position, or favor to behave nobly, kindly, and responsibly toward others.

The idea, of course, did not originate with the Frenchman.

---

[8]John 14:6.
[9]1 Timothy 3:15.
[10]Matthew 28:18–20.
[11]See Matthew 16:18.

The ancient Greeks reflected such attitudes in their writings, as shown by Euripides—"The nobly born must nobly meet his fate"[12]—and by Sophocles—"Nobly to live, or else nobly to die, befits proud birth."[13]

Men have known almost instinctively that as accomplishment and position rise, so do responsibility and burden. With each achievement, society raises its expectation a notch.

With the British of the nineteenth century, the concept of *noblesse oblige* reached its zenith, sometimes for good, sometimes for not-so-good. Regardless of mistakes, the British nobility perceived that if they were to have their country houses and servants, their privileges and honors, they in turn had to be responsible for the working people.

In the case of Great Britian as a whole, she felt a responsibility for the entire world, a duty to Pax Brittania—the British peace— on every continent. She called it the burden of empire, sending young men and women to India and the four corners of the earth, challenging any she felt would disrupt the peace of the world.

In a pattern that would be repeated, Russia threatened to enter Afghanistan in the late nineteenth century as a move toward a warm-water port in the Middle East. The British, accepting the responsibility accompanying their position as the world's greatest power, challenged the Russians and prevailed. To them, it was *noblesse oblige*, protecting the people from invaders, pirates, and brigands. To others, it often was unadulterated colonialism, in which people were exploited, confined to subservience and poverty. Both views contained truth. Humility and purity, among other virtues, were lacking. Nonetheless, Victorian Britain instinctively realized that the Law of Responsibility was a foundational corollary to her preeminent position in the nineteenth-century world.

---

[12]Euripides, *Alcymene*, c 485–406 B.C.
[13]Sophocles, *Ajax*, c.495–405 B.C.

The U.S. Faltered

Contrasted with the British leaning toward *noblesse oblige* were the frequent failures of responsibility by the government of the United States during the second half of this century. To begin with, Americans during most of their history worked hard under the Law of Use. They were frugal, disciplined, and moral. Furthermore, they persevered, and following World War II became the strongest power on earth. With that stature came responsibility, especially, in my judgment, the responsibility to accomplish two goals: to order the world economy and to keep world peace.

On the first, we began to fail rapidly in the sixties, refusing to measure up to the responsibility. We were profligate in our spending, igniting the timebomb of inflation, which we exported overseas since every other currency was tied into the American dollar. We printed money faster and faster, sending more abroad than we got back through sales of our own goods, eventually reaching a point where more than $600 billion of our money was held in foreign banks. This showed little sense of duty, strength, courage, or determination.

In 1971, shirking our responsibility even more, we went off the gold standard, having little choice in light of overseas claims against our currency. Thus inflation exploded across the world.

Second, as the leader of the free world, we faltered in our duty to lead in keeping the peace. It became especially critical after the Vietnam debacle, in which our course cost us severely in morale, determination, economic strength, and lives of thousands of valiant youths. From that point on, our neglect went on the downhill slalom. We neglected to keep the peace in Africa, allowing the Communist-led world to take several countries in an unprecedented display of international burglary. We allowed similar conduct in Latin America, where Communists took over Nicaragua and moved upon El Salvador and other countries.

All of this merely solidified a trend that had been building momentum since the end of World War II. For multifaceted reasons, we Americans seem to have no stomach for the full burden of leadership and responsibility demanded of someone to whom much has been given. We apparently want the position of power but not all the sacrifices of duty that accompany it. Because of historical and cultural factors, we have not developed a national fiber of *noblesse oblige*.

Yet, God and man insist on it. The parable told by Jesus about the slave who was made steward over his master's possessions said this about failure to fulfill responsibility: " 'And that slave who knew his master's will and did not get ready or act in accord with his will, shall receive many lashes. . . .' "[14]

In the eighties we are experiencing the pains of our neglect, beleaguered at every turn.

The Issue of Capitalism

Although I believe communism and capitalism in their most extreme, secular manifestations are equally doomed to failure, likely to result in tragic dictatorship, I at the same time believe free enterprise is the economic system most nearly meeting humanity's God-given need for freedom in existence. When greed and materialism displace all spiritual and moral values, capitalism breaks down into ugliness.

In his instructive and provocative book, *Wealth and Poverty*,[15] widely circulated in the early days of the Reagan Administration, George Gilder makes a convincing argument that capitalism at least *sets out* to fulfill generally what I am calling the Laws of Reciprocity and Use.

---

[14]Luke 12:47.
[15]George Gilder, *Wealth and Poverty* (New York: Bantam, 1982), pp. 30,31ff.

151

"Giving is the vital impulse and moral center of capitalism," he argues, adding:

Capitalists are motivated not chiefly by the desire to consume wealth or indulge their appetites, but by the freedom and power to consummate their entrepreneurial ideas. Whether piling up coconuts or designing new computers, they are movers and shakers, doers and givers, obsessed with positive visions of change and opportunity. They are men with an urge to understand and act, to master something and transform it, to work out a puzzle and profit from it, to figure out a part of nature and society and turn it to the common good. They are inventors and explorers, boosters and problem solvers; they take infinite pains and they strike fast.

Then he drives to the heart of the criticism leveled at the capitalists—their preoccupation with money. But his answers are logical and need to be heard.

Are they greedier than doctors or writers or professors of sociology or assistant secretaries of energy or commissars of wheat? Yes, their goals seem more mercenary. But this is only because money is their very means of production. Just as the sociologist requires books and free time and the bureaucrat needs arbitrary power, the capitalist needs capital . . . Capitalists need capital to fulfill their role in launching and financing enterprise. Are they self-interested? Presumably. But the crucial fact about them is their deep interest and engagement in the world beyond themselves, impelled by their imagination, optimism and faith.

His assessment is on target, I believe. Capitalism satisfies the freedom-loving side of humanity. It has an inherent quality of giving, of breaking through into new levels of experience. It uses that which it has and fully exploits the exponential curve, and perseverance is one of its tested virtues.

But what about responsibility? As success grows, the responsibility grows. Has the level of fulfillment of that responsibility kept pace? That is the problem.

His argument, while touching on "religious" factors, becomes muddy on the point of God and faith. He is imprecise, as in the case of the last word in the above-quoted passage. What precisely is the "faith" in? Everything else rests on that foundation. Imprecision will produce shakiness ultimately. Jesus said, " 'Have faith in God.' "[16] It was the umbrella for all activities.

If the faith is in God, then this quite naturally flavors the question of responsibility. Faith in God presumably will produce an acknowledgment of responsibility toward God—and an ongoing and rising responsibility toward men. This is where the capitalists most frequently stumble.

And they are not alone. Other conservatives have fallen short, too. This is exemplified by the evangelical Christians, who so often find themselves in league with economic and political conservatives. They have been given great understanding, and often they have given much in return. However, they have concentrated almost exclusively on personal salvation, neglecting responsibility for intelligent public policy, international affairs, the poor, the oppressed. To whom much enlightenment has been given, much will be required.

We in the developed world—capitalists, evangelicals, everyone—will be held accountable for all that has been given. The people in Africa and South America will not be held to the same level of accountability simply because they have not received as much.

Just think of the Western world! Think of the revelations in law, justice, science, medicine, technology, religion. Think of the rewards that have come through capitalism and evangelical Christianity, as merely two examples. Those revelations, those rewards, govern what is demanded of us—by God and by men.

The responsibility is great. And this may not be comprehended to the fullest by Gilder and his fellow conservatives

---

[16]Mark 11:22.

153 🦉

and capitalists. We all need to hear Isaiah, who in his great prophecy spelled out this responsibility, mincing no words in reporting God's instructions. We will look at only one section of them,[17] for they alone are enough to set us in motion with the Law of Responsibility.

Shout with the voice of a trumpet blast, tell my people of their sins! Yet they act so pious! They come to the Temple every day and are so delighted to hear the reading of my laws—just as though they would obey them—just as though they don't despise the commandments of their God! How anxious they are to worship correctly; oh, how they love the Temple services!

The words echo throughout the New Testament. How God deplores those who hear His word and dó not *do* it![18] They wonder why they don't see power in their lives. Isaiah looks at the kinds of questions they throw at God.

"We have fasted before you," they say. "Why aren't you impressed? Why don't you see our sacrifices? Why don't you hear our prayers? We have done much penance, and you don't even notice it!" I'll tell you why! Because you are living in evil pleasure even while you are fasting, and *you keep right on oppressing your workers.* Look, what good is fasting when *you keep on fighting and quarreling?* This kind of fasting will never get you anywhere with me. . . .

No, the Lord says, your revelation carries a responsibility, to Him and to people. He hits the point on workers hard.

No, the kind of fast I want is that you stop *oppressing* those who work for you and treat them fairly and give them what they earn.

Then he broadens it.

---

[17]Isaiah 58:1–11, TLB.
[18]See James 1:22–25.

I want you to share your food with the hungry and bring right into your own homes those who are helpless, poor and destitute. Clothe those who are cold and don't hide from relatives who need your help.

Fulfill your responsibility at the level to which He has raised you, God says, and He will raise you even higher.

If you do these things, God will shed His own glorious light upon you. He will heal you; your godliness will lead you forward, and goodness will be a shield before you, and the glory of the Lord will protect you from behind. Then, when you call, the Lord will answer. "Yes, I am here," he will quickly reply. All you need to do is to stop oppressing the weak, and to stop making false accusations and spreading vicious rumors!

From the beginning of the Scriptures to the end, a theme flows relentlessly: *God is the enemy of oppression.* So must His people be. In His behalf, Isaiah pounds at the issues even more boldly.

Feed the hungry! Help those in trouble! . . . And the Lord will . . . satisfy you with all good things . . . and you will be like a well-watered garden, like an ever-flowing spring.

Give, and it will be given to you. Fulfill your responsibility at your current level if you would rise to a higher one. Blessing carries responsibility.

Unending commitment to that truth would advance the cause of capitalism and free enterprise immensely, carrying it perhaps past the dangers of anarchy and dictatorship. It would also advance the cause of evangelical Christianity, perhaps to the point of winning the world, a feat that has thus far eluded us.

155

ELEVEN
THE LAW OF GREATNESS

꿰 All people desire to be great.

Because of human frailty, however, this can turn out badly, especially if we think in terms of comparison with others, for that usually spells pride.

But to think more deeply than that is possible. Pride is still a hazard, but one can set goals of accomplishing tasks rather than of performing better than someone else. It's a fine line, but it exists.

Jesus, pointing to that line, spoke of the possibilities of greatness—a purity of greatness, we might say. Indeed, He set forth a two-part principle that I have labeled the Law of Greatness. The world needs it desperately at this hour.

It is easy to forget that the people surrounding Jesus during His earthly ministry were just that—people. Plain, simple, ordinary people. They exhibited the frailties of all of us. For example, at one point, acting a bit like twentieth-century kids quarreling over who's the greatest shortstop in the American League, the disciples came to the Lord and asked, " 'Who then is the greatest in the kingdom of heaven?' "

The answer was remarkable, flying in the face of everything we expect in our day.

And He called a child to Himself and set him before them, and said, "Truly I say to you, unless you are converted and become like children, you shall not enter the kingdom of heaven. Whoever then humbles himself as this child, *he is the greatest in the kingdom of heaven.*"[1]

At another time, they fell into a dispute over which of *them* was regarded as the greatest. They, like us, were very concerned about their status from time to time. But the Lord showed great patience with them.

And He said to them, "The kings of the Gentiles lord it over them; and those who have authority over them are called 'Benefactors.' But not so with you, but *let him who is the greatest among you become as the youngest, and the leader as the servant.* For who is greater, the one who reclines at the table, or the one who serves? Is it not the one who reclines at the table? But I am among you as *the one who serves.*"[2]

Every time the question arose, the answer was the same two-pronged directive: If you want to be great, become like a *child* and become a *servant.* And that answer reverberates down through human experience to our day, yet so few of us grasp it.

"Oh, that was OK for what He was doing then," we say, "but He didn't understand what it was going to be like in the modern world."

Or we mumble something like, "That may be all right for church, but you'll get killed in the real world."

---

[1] Matthew 18:2–4.
[2] Luke 22:25–27.

157

If you're honest, you have to admit those remarks seem true as the twentieth century winds down. Knowledge has exploded all over the planet and even onto other planets; man is doing things never dreamed possible. Furthermore, we are in a life-and-death struggle for minds and bodies. Greatness will be measured by success in that explosion and struggle. A little child won't stand a chance.

We all rationalize that way. And we are all in a mess as a result. We should look at what Jesus was showing us.

What is there about a little child that He wants us to copy? If they're very little, they cry a lot and seem to be pretty much governed by what their stomachs tell them. If they have pain, they cry; if they're wet, they cry. As they grow, they're apt to be spoiled by their families. They may become extraordinarily self-centered; they may whine a lot. In time, they may become unruly and undisciplined. All parents know the pattern.

Is this what Jesus wanted us to be?

No, He had something else in mind. He spoke of three qualities that under normal circumstances predominate in little children: They are trusting. They are teachable. They are humble.

To begin with, little children trust their mothers and fathers. They have to. A baby relies upon his mother to feed him, trusting that she is not going to put poison in his mouth. As he grows, he believes in his parents, usually certain that his daddy is absolutely the greatest man in the world. We all know that many things can work to warp that trust, but basically all children, if treated the way God would have parents treat their offspring, will have incredible faith in their mothers and fathers. They won't worry about being fed, clothed, or housed. They will simply trust that their parents will meet their needs.

Such total trust in the provision and protection of God is the first giant step toward greatness.

As for being teachable, children, most significantly, will listen.

They have voracious appetites for learning, and, since they're starting from zero, they know the best way to feed those appetites is to listen. They may ask a lot of questions, but they listen to the answers. "Daddy, why is the grass green? Daddy, why are the birds flying? Daddy, why is the car running?"

It never stops. Their minds are set in the inquiry mode.

Too often parents become annoyed, but they need to understand that this is a mark of intelligence. It is desirable and pleasing to the Creator. A child between the ages of four and five will learn more in that one year than a student will in four years of college.

This teachableness has an interesting side effect that I'm sure Jesus had in mind. Children, hungry to learn, will experiment. They are quick to master new ideas, new languages, new techniques. Their minds are open. If we think of this in the context of God's instructions to Adam and Eve to master and subdue the earth,[3] we see the importance of such inquiry and openness.

They are steps toward greatness.

Then, little children are humble—at least until someone spoils them. You seldom see a young child vaunting himself like something special. This virtue is eventually corrupted by a society that has become increasingly warped through the centuries, but in his very early years a child doesn't care if his dad is a prince or a pauper, highly educated or lacking in training. All he cares is that that man is daddy and he loves him. Usually this carries over to attitudes toward others; he loves people as people, regardless of social status.

Quite simply, children love life, until we train this quality out of them. When you watch them play, they are free; they throw themselves into situations with abandon, even getting a little reckless. And they'll throw themselves into your arms with absolute delight. While fully content in the fact that their parents are

---

[3]See Genesis 1:28.

sovereign—it's so good and natural that they never even think to challenge it—they are free to be free.

They wear no masks. They're innocent, transparent, and genuine. Become like them and you're on the road to greatness.

The New Testament is jammed with urgings toward humility, and we have noted the importance of this virtue in simply moving toward the kingdom of God. But we should observe that Jesus, in a parallel passage on greatness, reemphasized that insistence on humility. It is a virtue with more than passing importance. After having said that " 'the greatest among you shall be your servant,' "[4] He continued: " 'And whoever exalts himself shall be humbled; and *whoever humbles himself shall be exalted.*' "[5]

With that principle, Christ was pointing to a truth that Solomon had unfolded in a different way: "The reward of humility and the fear of the LORD/Are riches, honor and life."[6] Greatness, summed up as "riches, honor and life," is the reward of those who are humble, which is the necessary ingredient for fearing the Lord. And that, psychology confirms, is what men long for—financial reward, recognition, and a good, satisfying life. It all awaits the little child, epitome of the humble.

So, in short, Jesus said greatness begins with being trusting, being teachable, and being humble. The three traits go together—not merely in children, but in adults as well. The trusting person puts away cynicism and skepticism, and becomes open. He doesn't have to be right all the time. Then he is able to learn—from God, from people, from circumstances. He'll listen; he'll try new things. And *that* is the humble person.

Do you see the circle? Trust. Teachableness. Humility. They run from one to another, backward and forward.

The businessman who becomes like a child in this regard will rise to greatness. So will the scientist. So will the minister.

[4]Matthew 18:4 (paraphrased).
[5]Matthew 23:12.
[6]Proverbs 22:4.

A Difficult Concept

In the second episode we examined at the beginning of this chapter, Jesus added another criterion for greatness. Quite paradoxically, He said the secret of greatness is service. If you reflect on it, you see that it fits well with being childlike, but it begins to rub. It goes against the grain of society.

That is why we should be serious and careful on this subject. We are dealing with a law that turns everything upside down. Little children soon yearn to grow up so they can "be somebody." But Jesus says, "Be a child if you really want to *be* somebody." Servants, meanwhile, usually hate their position, yearning to earn enough to have their *own* servants. But Jesus says, "No, become a servant if you wish to be truly great."

This pushes us into a corner where we have to ask, "Do I really want this?" We should weigh it carefully, for the Lord said to count the cost of the things we set out to do.[7]

If you're an average workingman, you may have been striving all your life to escape any image of servanthood, trying to rise to the point, perhaps, where you work for yourself and not for someone else.

If you're a black man or woman, you've known the effects of the struggle against slavery all your life, and the most onerous recollection you have is your race's all-too-frequent relegation to the role of household servant. Can anyone challenge the black's desire to attain to the higher professions and cast off once and for all the idea of serving someone?

If you've experienced management-labor relations, you understand that no manager has any true desire to be a servant of the labor ranks, and no laboring man will accept the slightest hint

---

[7]See Luke 14:28.

that he's a servant of management or anyone else. Such thinking is anathema to both parties.

If you're a politician, you smile indulgently when someone refers to you as a "public servant;" you really prefer the role of celebrity.

If you're a minister of the gospel, "successful" and well-known on the speaking circuit or perhaps on television, the chances are great that you're far more comfortable signing autographs and sitting at headtables than being a servant to the flock.

You see, there will be a cost if we seek true greatness. For our attitudes—wrong ones—are well solidified, despite the fact that we have had examples of true greatness over the years.

My generation considered Albert Schweitzer to be a great man, and most—even those who disagreed with his theology—would acknowledge that his was true greatness. Why? Because he became like a little child and like a servant. He gave his life for the sick, the oppressed. He was trusting, teachable, and humble. He was a servant.

A scientist, musician, philosopher, and theologian, he left what the world would have considered to be the road to greatness in Germany and went to Africa to labor among primitive, under-privileged people in a little village. Establishing a hospital, he lived his life out in full service to others, continually learning, continually enthusiastic, continually innocent.

Even the modern world came to understand that his greatness was somehow different from the greatness most men sought. Year after year, he was numbered at the top of the list of outstanding people.

Similarly, polls measuring the ten most admired women in the world place a remarkable Roman Catholic nun, Mother Theresa of Calcutta, at the top. This is a woman who has given up everything, in a materialistic world's terms, to go among the poor, downtrodden masses of India to feed them, clothe them, house them, and love them.

Hers is a role of a servant through and through, a refusal to lord it over anyone, and yet we somehow know she has achieved greatness.

Stepping back through history, we encounter Father Damien, the Belgian priest who gave himself entirely to service to the leper colony on the Hawaiian island of Molokai in the mid-nineteenth century. His was true greatness.

And there is Hudson Taylor, the missionary who turned away from a life of comfort in Britain to throw himself into service of the suffering and lost Chinese. His greatness still rings in the annals of missionary service.

And there was Florence Nightingale, the English nurse who served heroically in the Crimean War and became known as the founder of modern nursing.

These unusual humanitarians were among those who found the key to success through the Law of Greatness.

It Works in Business

The business world, too, has produced greatness. And we need to understand that the principles set forth by Jesus are pragmatic and effective in the hard-nosed give-and-take of free enterprise.

Henry Ford was a good illustration. He wanted to make inexpensive, efficient transportation available to as many people as possible. So he came up with the Model T. Before long he was serving thousands with cheap transportation. The more he served, the more money he made, and the greater his business became. He became the greatest figure in the auto industry.

The Law of Greatness did not gain a permanent foothold in the American car industry, however. Confrontation gradually replaced service. Management and labor lost all semblance of unity, and the thought of serving one another became a joke. The industry also confronted the public, steadily losing awareness about changes in society, consumer economics, and fuel outlook. It designed cars the way *it* wanted them.

The early tolling of the death bell went largely unnoticed.

Eventually deterioration in the concept of service reached a point where car manufacturers decided that fully effective quality control at the factories was too expensive. Their surveys convinced them that they would be better off to repair mistakes at the dealership level.

So the cars came off the line with little things untended. The buyers drove them a short while and something would malfunction. When they took them back, the dealers made the repairs and sent the bill to the manufacturer. Almost inevitably something else would happen to the same car, and the process would be repeated. It was terribly inconvenient for car buyers, but it was less expensive for the manufacturer.

The tolling of the bell grew louder as the principle of service fell by the roadside.

This, as we noted in an earlier chapter, was not the case in Japan. There, thoughts of service penetrated deeper into the industrial consciousness. The desire grew to end shoddiness and to give customers the best products on the road. The industry would serve the people.

Secondly, management and labor began to work at the idea of becoming servants of one another. Companies took pains to instill in their managers the thought that they were servants of the workers. "We're here to make their jobs better, to improve their environment, to solve their problems," they repeated. Furthermore, they became like little children and listened to their workers. "We want to learn from you," management said, and before long workers were each submitting eighteen or nineteen suggestions a year for improving the work process; and management was adopting at least 80 percent.

The employees, meanwhile, were constantly reinforced in their understanding, through attitudes and material rewards, that they were servants of the customers and the society.

Serving is a concept that works at every level, even in an enterprise as massive as the automobile industry of a major, very prosperous nation. For, as the world knows, the Japanese auto industry overwhelmed everyone, even gaining a foothold in America that resulted in a major share of sales.

The principle works in other industries, too. J. C. Penney, for example, embraced the concept of giving a square deal to everyone—honest merchandise, honest measure, honest price. With that in mind, he developed a giant chain of stores across America, becoming a great man in merchandising.

It Is Needed Now

So a life principle emerges. Those who serve others—whether in religion, philanthrophy, education, science, art, government, or business—are the great ones. Indeed, the deeper the sacrifice or the broader the scope of service, the greater the individual becomes.

And rarely will our society award the status of greatness to those who lust for personal power and seek to exalt themselves. How often we hear applied to such persons the phrases "petty tyrant . . . little Caesar . . . self-seeking . . . ruthless . . . vain." And though occasionally these people rise to prominence, they never touch greatness. Invariably the Law of Reciprocity brings them down.

Looking around us in the eighties, we would probably find a consensus that if ever greatness was needed in the world, it is now. We have few statesmen of international stature, for example. Instead of greatness of spirit, we find meanness. Our vision is dim.

We frankly need leadership at every level, especially in the international realm, as Armageddon looms closer with each passing day. We need men and women to lead our nation in taking on the responsibilities and the risks of serving other nations, helping

165

them to achieve their potential, helping them with education, agriculture, and industry. We need to cast off paternalism and exploitation.

We need to dare to live the Beatitudes at this level, to be trusting, teachable, and humble, to discover perhaps for the first time in history how a man who is a servant can lead.

In addition to being spiritually and biblically sound, this course has a very practical result. The nation that does the most for others will be the one growing in greatness, the one other nations, as customers, will turn to, the one whose products will sweep around the world. That nation will be exalted, elevated, enlarged as the Laws of Reciprocity and Use take hold.

As with nations, so with all of us.

TWELVE

THE LAW OF UNITY

🜪 From the beginning of His revelation to mankind, God has held forth a difficult principle that flows naturally into and out of the concept of serving. Men have continually stumbled over it.

I call it the Law of Unity. It is simple to understand, and devastatingly difficult to obey. But it is essential. God has been trying to explain that to us for thousands of years.

Unity is central to the way the world works. Perhaps the most powerful illustration of that is found in God Himself, in the Bible's account of creation. "Then God said, 'Let *Us* make man in *Our* image, according to *Our* likeness. . . .'"[1]

This is the only part of the Creation where such language is used and, admittedly, we don't know with great precision what the Lord was inspiring the writer to communicate. He probably

---

[1]Genesis 1:26.

was referring to the Godhead, the Trinity, when He spoke of "Us." But He could have been speaking of the angelic court of God or perhaps even the multifaceted majesty of God. Regardless, there was some form of conversation involving more than one Person, and *there was unity.*

Although the passage presents many significant facts, this is the one we should see here: Within the Godhead (or the court of heaven) there was agreement and harmony. God moves in unity.

Thus, the principle is first stated: Great creativity occurs where there is unity. God's unfathomable power is released where there is harmony.

The early Genesis accounts add another piece of insight in this regard. After man had refused to obey God and live under His sovereignty, the half-truth of Satan, the liar and deceiver, came to pass: Adam and Eve became " 'like God.' "[2] We are not able to comprehend the seriousness of that moment. It was history's terrible tragedy. Man, the delight of God's heart, had fallen. And we read these words:

Then the LORD God said, "Behold, the man has become like one of *Us,* knowing good and evil; and now, lest he stretch out his hand, and take also from the tree of life, and eat, and live forever"— therefore the LORD God sent him out from the garden of Eden. . . .[3]

Judgment flowed from unity. Just as the magnificent power of creation had sprung from the perfect harmony of heaven, so had the dreadful power of judgment and justice come from the awesome unity of the Almighty.

The examples are clear. God moves in unity. Harmony is central to the unleashing of God's incredible power.

Furthermore, unity in the invisible world governs the visible

---

[2]Genesis 3:5.
[3]Genesis 3:22,23.

world. If it works in heaven, it works on earth. " 'Thy kingdom come. Thy will be done. *On earth as it is in heaven.*' "[4]

This operation of the Law of Unity on earth was the point of one of the Lord's most-quoted statements:

"Again I say to you, that if *two of you agree on earth about anything* that they may ask, *it shall be done* for them by My Father who is in heaven. For where two or three have gathered together in My name, there I am in their midst."[5]

He was calling for agreement, but not merely for agreement's sake. He was calling for unity. Since He would be in their midst when they gathered to consider some issue, they would be expected to agree with Him. Their unity would be an external manifestation of their internal agreement. Since He was there, He would bring them to harmony if they genuinely laid aside their own preconceptions and centered on Him.

Then, and only then, would power flow, just as at the Creation. For unity is the fountainhead of God's creative power.

There is a multiplication factor in that unity too. We see it in a song of Moses spoken to all of Israel as he approached the end of his life. One standing on the Rock, he said, would chase a thousand of the enemy, while two would put ten thousand to flight.[6] Unity does not cause a mere doubling or tripling of power; the progression explodes.

The Early Church

The biblical accounts of unity within the early church show the power of the Law of Unity. For example, the fledgling

---

[4]Matthew 6:10.
[5]Matthew 18:19,20.
[6]See Deuteronomy 32:30.

assembly (the *ekklesia* or church) continued to stick together after Christ's crucifixion, resurrection, and ascension—still weak, still uncertain, still afraid. But an enlightening verse says, "These all *with one mind* were continually devoting themselves to prayer. . . ."[7] They were in accord in unity.

Then, the Bible says, power flowed through and from that unity. The Holy Spirit, the giver of life and power, was sent forth upon the people of God as never before. The church was on its way.

At another critical stage, we see the launching of the missionary outreach that was to change the world as the people reached unity and harmony. This occurred in Antioch, where the Lord's followers were first called Christians.[8]

Now there were at Antioch, in the church that was there, prophets and teachers: Barnabas, and Simeon who was called Niger, and Lucius of Cyrene, and Manaen who had been brought up with Herod the tetrarch, and Saul. And while they were ministering to the Lord and fasting, the Holy Spirit said, "Set apart for Me Barnabas and Saul for the work to which I have called them." Then, when they had fasted and prayed and laid their hands on them, they sent them away.[9]

The Lord acted in that setting of harmony, in which those great and diverse leaders centered in on Christ—"ministering" to Him, worshiping Him, turning their full devotion upon Him, feasting upon Him rather than upon ordinary food. He called out Saul,whose name was changed to Paul,[10] and Barnabas, the "Son of Encouragement" whose name had already been changed from Joseph, and sent them forth in power.[11]

---

[7]Acts 1:14.
[8]See Acts 11:26.
[9]Acts 13:1–3.
[10]See Acts 13:1,9.
[11]See Acts 4:33,36.

We see in all of these reports evidence that people will not hear the voice of God clearly unless the unity of the Spirit is maintained. Disunity will cause the Spirit to flee.

If we need further support for the point, we have only to look at the recent history of the church. Division and disunity have been its most distinguishing characteristics, with the result that it has been impotent to move the world. It has lacked the power that flows from unity. It is small wonder that Jesus, on the night of his betrayal, prayed so movingly and powerfully for the harmony of His people, asking that they might be " 'perfected in unity.' "[12] He knew how critical it was.

For Good or For Evil

A fascinating aspect of unity is that it apparently generates a power that can work for good or for evil, at least for a time. We find this illustrated early in the Bible in the story of the Tower of Babel.

After the Flood, we read, "the whole earth used the same language and the same words."[13] The people were becoming gradually unified and beginning to work in harmony. They discovered the use of bricks and mortar, for example, and set out to build themselves a city with a great tower "whose top will reach into heaven" They wanted to make "a name" for themselves and to grow as a unified force.[14]

If we read carefully, we see that their motive reflected pride. Their plan actually constituted man's first effort to glorify himself. They wanted to build a memorial to themselves, a symbolic assault on heaven in defiance of God.

---

[12]John 17:23.
[13]Genesis 11:1.
[14]Genesis 11:4.

God viewed this as sin, and Scripture records His reaction as follows:

". . . Behold, they are *one people*, and they all have the same language. And this is what they began to do, and now *nothing which they purpose to do will be impossible* for them. Come, let Us go down and there confuse their language, that they may not understand one another's speech." So the LORD scattered them abroad from there over the face of the whole earth. . . .[15]

God Almighty saw that the people were of one mind and one language; they were unified. Nothing would be impossible for them, whether for good or for evil.

God's assessment is blunt: Mankind in unity becomes absolutely overwhelming.

There are those who might think God's action against Babel was harsh and unreasonable, so we must make sure we comprehend the truth of the episode. The Lord instantly understood that the people's intention was to unify in glorifying man, which meant the same thing as unifying in rebellion against God. The Bible, as we have seen, tells us that God resists the proud but gives favor to the humble. Indeed, He resists pride in any form. Any expression of rebellious pride, especially the pride of a unified group, wherever found, will ultimately draw opposition from Him.

It is noteworthy that pride, which leads to the glorification of man, continues in the world today in a subtler, yet similar manner. It goes under the label of secular humanism, which, in truth, is a religion of man. Its intention is to build great towers, as it were, to the glory of man. Moving slowly, but persistently, across the earth and capitalizing on the natural pride of man, it has been gaining adherents. Its final aim is the rejection of the centrality of God and the removal of religious freedom from society. The

---

[15]Genesis 11:6–8.

unity of its believers has given it unprecedented force in our time.

Bible believers draw confidence, however, from the fact that the Scripture announces that such forces as those gathered under the banner of humanism or those who rallied at Babel, as long as they remain in opposition to God, will be defeated. The Bible places them under the name of "Babylon," which is doomed to annihilation.[16] It is noteworthy that the presumed site of the Tower of Babel was at or near historical Babylon.

The lesson we are to learn from all of this is that the Lord God takes the matter of unity very seriously. We, His people, should do no less.

Unity of Quest

Unity must begin with the individual. If you are going to experience the power that can change the world, you must be unified within yourself. You must have internal harmony. In the Bible, James addresses this point specifically. A "double-minded man," he says, will not receive anything from the Lord.[17]

One mind believing or desiring one thing and in the same person another mind believing or desiring something else will not work. And there can be no doubting, James added, ". . . for the one who doubts is like the surf of the sea driven and tossed by the wind."[18]

Instead, the Bible says, you must be as Abraham was when, at a hundred years of age and sonless, he was told he would be the father of many nations. He did not "waver" regarding the promise, but remained fully assured that God would perform what He had said.[19]

---

[16]See Revelation 14:8.
[17]James 1:6–8.
[18]James 1:6.
[19]See Romans 4:13–21.

Abraham had unified his quest in life. He did not fall victim to spiritual schizophrenia, which wracks so many in their walk with the Lord. People can be torn between the pursuit of worldly goals and the pursuit of the Christian life. They can't make up their minds which to put first, needing desperately to hear the words of David: "My heart is fixed, O God, my heart is fixed . . . ."[20]

The well-known story of Mary and Martha illustrates the problem.

Now as they were traveling along, He entered a certain village; and a woman named Martha welcomed Him into her home. And she had a sister called Mary, who moreover was listening to the Lord's word, seated at His feet. But Martha was distracted with all her preparations; and she came up to Him, and said, "Lord, do You not care that my sister has left me to do all the serving alone? Then tell her to help me." But the Lord answered and said to her, "Martha, Martha, you are worried and bothered about so many things; but only a few things are necessary, really only one, for Mary has chosen the good part, which shall not be taken away from her."[21]

We must not interpret that passage as approval of laziness or irresponsibility. Jesus loved Martha and her willingness to serve, but He was concerned about her attitude, her internal unity. Mary had " 'chosen the good part' "; her quest had been unified. If need be, she would sacrifice all else for it. But Martha wanted to be recognized as a follower of Jesus *and* as a good organizer *and* as a good cook. She wasn't single-minded, and she had no peace. She was " 'worried and bothered about so many things.' "

We cannot serve two masters.[22] We can not put our spouse and Jesus first in our lives at the same time. We cannot put our job

---

[20]Psalm 57:7, KJV.
[21]Luke 10:38–42.
[22]See Matthew 6:24.

ahead of everything and serve Jesus as Lord at the same time. Our problem is that we make a gap between the two, seeing them as two masters, and try to put each one first. That leads to schizophrenia and breakdowns.

The solution, of course, is to be single-minded. Put Jesus first, and then He will say, "Love your wife as I loved the church."[23] A spouse can get no greater love than that. Similarly, put Jesus first and He will say, "When you undertake a task, do it with all your might."[24] A job can get no more attention than that.

Single-mindedness is the solution to the internal desperation so many people regularly experience. It removes the terrible burden and dark heaviness that weigh upon the chest as they teeter on the fringes of nervous collapse.

A Collective Principle Also

The Bible is precise in showing that what is true for the individual is true for the family, the group, the organization, and the nation. When the Pharisees accused Him of being in league with Satan, Jesus countered with the following universal principle: ". . . 'Any kingdom divided against itself is laid waste; and any city or house divided against itself shall not stand.'"[25]

His point was simple. Without internal unity in a group—whether a family, a business, or a political entity—that group will ultimately collapse. Vacillation and dissension will lead to tearing and destruction.

Jesus, in this verse, was talking about the kingdom of Satan, showing that such universal principles as the Law of Unity apply everywhere. They are broader than religion. Even works of evil will collapse unless the evil forces are unified.

---

[23]See Ephesians 5:25.
[24]Ecclesiastes 9:10 (paraphrased).
[25]Matthew 12:25.

Unity produces strength; disunity produces weakness. Obviously, this was not a New Testament revelation. The Lord's words quickly remind us of the teachings of the man credited with unimaginable wisdom, Solomon: "He who troubles his own house will inherit wind. . . ."[26] This proverb was thoroughly supported throughout biblical history. Houses of leadership would often fall to scheming and fighting among themselves, and then the leadership would crumble.

In my generation, the name of Kennedy immediately comes to mind when we consider the strength derived from unity within a house or clan. Working together and for the good of the family or for one of its members, the Kennedys of Massachusetts achieved remarkable political success. The power of the individual was geometrically multiplied by the harmony of the group. We have fewer and fewer examples of such family unity.

The same is true of the business world. We need only think of those businessess that have fallen on hard times because they abandoned clear-cut unity of mission in favor of diversification. A great electronics company foundered because it tried to make large computers. A chemical company ran into trouble when it tried to be a land developer.

Successful organizations, as well as successful individuals, are those unified around a relatively simple statement of goals and mission. A double-minded man is "unstable in all his ways."[27] So is a double-minded business.

At the national level, the problem is just as great. Turning back into history we see the roots of modern-day Italy, whose turmoil may be greater than any developed country in the world despite its conspicuous marks of great civilization. Before the time of Garibaldi's efforts to unify Italy in the nineteenth century, that

------

[26]Proverbs 11:29.
[27]James 1:8.

land witnessed the struggle of little city-states to prevail over one another and maintain their autonomy. Garibaldi brought them together in a fragile alliance; but following the wars in our century and the conditions in modern Europe, Italy is probably best described as "the sick man" of the continent, owing almost exclusively to the absence of harmony.

The factions in that nation simply will not come together. The house is divided. Consequently, the economy is sick; the society with its unbelievable terrorism and crime is unstable; governmental services falter. Life is a shambles.

In the United States, the history is different and the symptoms vary, but the disease is the same. From its founding until about 1960, Americans were united by at least a common ethic. Essentially, the country had been founded as a Christian nation, adopting biblical principles and governing itself pretty much under biblical countenance. There was a work ethic and moral restraint based on an underlying philosophical system of honor and decency that prevailed even in the face of frequent and flagrant violations.

Today, the United States struggles under a social philosophy of pluralism. There is no unified reality. Many disparate, frequently cacophonous voices echo from one shore to another. Confusion is triumphant.

A "700 Club" guest once asked a question typically heard in the current atmosphere: "Whatever happened to the concept that 'I am my brother's keeper'?"

The answer was easy. It vanished with the Christian ethic. Such concepts spring from a God-centered society, but we no longer have that unifying force. We now are fragmented, and each fragment spawns its own jealousy and self-concern. If this continues and the rival factions increase and strengthen, the country will fall quite simply from violation of the Law of Unity.

Unity With Diversity

It is important we understand that unity springing from the truth of the kingdom of God does not insist on, or even desire, uniformity. Lessons from the Bible about the unity of the Godhead make this abundantly clear. There is diversity even with the oneness of the Trinity.

We see this point in the lives of Christ's disciples, too. They were unified in their quest; but they were a diverse lot, thoroughly nonconformist in several instances.

Paul the apostle taught on this in a spiritual lesson that has physical applications:

Now there are *varieties* of gifts, but the same Spirit. And there are *varieties* of ministries, and the same Lord. And there are *varieties* of effects, but the same God who works all things in all persons. But to each one is given the manifestation of the Spirit for the common good.[28]

Variety is God's way, he said, even invoking the Trinity to make the point—Spirit, Lord, God. Variety and diversity serve God's purpose, working distinctively and pointedly to arrive at the common good.

No, in families, businesses, churches, and nations, the Lord is not seeking a collection of robots. He is seeking people with varying personalities, talents, and styles who are unified in purpose and will work toward the common good.

Using His principles harmoniously, they can overcome the crises of our century.

Keenly aware of this the night before He was crucified, Jesus prayed to His Father in this manner:

"I do not ask in behalf of these alone, but for those also who believe in Me through their word; *that they may all be one;* even as

---

[28]1 Corinthians 12:4–7.

Thou, Father, art in Me, and I in Thee, that they also may be in Us; that the world may believe that Thou didst send Me. And the glory which Thou hast given Me I have given to them; *that they may be one, just as We are one;* I in them, and Thou in Me, that they may be perfected in unity, that the world may know that Thou didst send Me, and didst love them, even as Thou didst love Me."[29]

He knew that the fulfillment of the purposes of God would require unity. Without it, there would be no flow of power to save the world and to perfect the people of God.

---

[29]John 17:20–23.

THIRTEEN

THE LAW OF MIRACLES

᪐ᦂ᪐ Now to the miraculous.

We have seen how the kingdom works.

We have looked briefly at how our physical world appears to be approaching the outer limits of survival through its violation of the laws of the spiritual world on which everything we know ultimately stands.

We have considered how the invisible nature of that spiritual world does not diminish its reality, but merely governs who will understand it.

We have spoken of reaching into that spiritual world, touching the truth and power of God, and transferring them into the physical world. This is possible even as we hurtle toward that moment when the kingdom of God will burst into visibility and supplant all the kingdoms and powers on earth.

It is this point of reaching into the invisible and seeing its effects manifest in the visible that we should examine more closely. There is a Law of Miracles. It governs the question of God's willingness to disrupt His natural order to accomplish His purpose. When He does disrupt that natural order, the result is a miracle, a contravention of the natural laws through which He usually works moment by moment. He overrides the way in which things normally operate.

Since God is almighty, the only absolutely free person in the universe, not bound even by His own creation, He is perfectly able at any time to change the way things are done. He can heal a body instantly; He can still a storm, and He can move a mountain. Those are miracles.

Even then, however, He works within principles, and they frame the Law of Miracles.

Because of the desperate condition of our world, we still need miracles today. That means we need to understand the law and act on it, for Jesus introduced a new order of normality at the Day of Pentecost. With the power of the Holy Spirit, miracles were to be normal. He expected His followers to do even greater things than He did.[1] After all, during His incarnation He rebuked them for failing to do miracles like walking on water and casting out demons. And He praised an outsider, A Roman centurion, who perceived Christ's spiritual authority and discerned the relationship between the spiritual and the natural. "Just say the word and my servant will be healed," the centurion declared.

Jesus marveled at the Roman's understanding. " '. . . I have not found such great faith with anyone in Israel,'" He said.[2]

That is what we must recover.

---

[1]See John 14:12.
[2]Matthew 8:10.

The Umbrella of Faith

"Have faith in God."[3] In chapter four, we saw that to understand how the kingdom works, we have to *begin* there. That was the umbrella given by Jesus in explaining the cursing of the fig tree. We have to *end* there, too.

Through the process of rebirth—by grace through faith—we are to see and enter into the kingdom of heaven, where the miraculous power resides. As the Lord explained to Nicodemus, this is the world of the Spirit, which is like the wind, invisible, yet frequently revealing its effects. We cannot see the wind itself, but we can see the things it moves. With the kingdom, we too observe its effects. Furthermore, we gain access to its power through our faith in Jesus Christ, through our rebirth.

We might think of ourselves as a people dying of thirst. But off in a distance there is a pool of water, a reservoir with a dam and beautiful pebble-lined banks. We can see the green trees and lush grass in its vicinity, but we can't see the reservoir itself. We desperately need to get to it.

By accepting Jesus, all that He is, all that He has done—by being born again—we gain access to this marvelous reservoir, this thirst-quenching pool of water, the kingdom of God. We are given access to an entirely new world, a heretofore invisible world—the secret kingdom.

"Have faith in God," Jesus said. Believe that God exists, trust Him, expect Him to enter into communion with you, to show you His will and purpose. Use the water in the reservoir. Remember that faith is the title deed to that pool of power.

It is all ours, if we know the *rules of miracles*.

First, we are to take our eyes off the circumstances and the impossibilities and to look upon God and the possibilities.

We have good examples from the history of God's people for

---

[3]Mark 11:22.

this. Remember Joshua and Caleb.[4] Representing the twelve tribes of Israel, they and ten others were sent as spies to determine if the people should enter into the land promised to them by God. They stayed forty days and returned with reports of a marvelous land of milk and honey, but it was peopled with giants living in fortified cities.

"They are too strong for us," ten of the spies said.

But Caleb and Joshua, who were to figure prominently in Israel's future, were enthusiastic and eager to move ahead. "It doesn't matter how many giants there are. The Lord is with us." They looked at God and not at the circumstances, reflecting the attitude He expected of His people.

Yet the ten others prevailed, exploiting the fears of the Israelites existing since their flight from Egypt. They succumbed to their crisis, ignoring the principles of the miraculous, and failed to take what was theirs.

The biblical story of Jonathan, the son of King Saul, shows us how to focus on God rather than circumstances.[5] He and his young armor-bearer, looking at a great field of enemy Philistine soldiers, put out a sign to see if God was with them. He was. So they moved to the attack, declaring that it was no harder for the Lord to win with a few than with many. Their refusal to be deterred by seemingly impossible circumstances led to an important victory by the entire army of Israel.

Second, we are not to doubt in our hearts.

We have seen that spirit controls matter, that lesser authority yields to greater authority, and that the mind and the voice are the instruments by which the will of the spirit is transmitted to the environment.

For miracles to happen through us, God's will must first be transmitted by the Holy Spirit to our spirits. Then, Jesus de-

---

[4]See Numbers 13,14.
[5]See 1 Samuel 14:1–15.

clared, we must not doubt in our hearts. The inmost center of our beings—which the Bible alternately terms the "heart" or the "spirit"—must be focused on the objective. Our hearts must be fully persuaded, without any doubt. We must be like Abraham, who against all hope believed God would grant him a son by his wife Sarah. "He staggered not at the promise of God through unbelief; but was strong in faith, giving glory to God; and being fully persuaded that, what he had promised, he was able also to perform."[6]

In fact, the persuasion in our spirit must be so strong that it seems to us the desired result has already taken place. As Jesus put it, "believe that you have received" and you will have what you say.

I experienced this extraordinary *present* possession of a *future* miracle before I acquired CBN's first television station. Although my available capital was only $70, and I was without a job, and although I did not own a television set and was without any knowledge of broadcasting, motion pictures, or theater, the purchase of a station became for me a present reality. Even now it is hard to describe my inner experience at that time. The persuasion in my spirit was so real that purchasing a station with $70 seemed as possible as buying a bag of groceries at a supermarket.

As an official of RCA later told me, "You sounded so positive that we thought you had the money in the bank."

To those around me who could see only the *visible* reality, I was on a fool's errand. The things I was attempting were clearly impossible. But God had given me a measure of faith, and my spirit counted God's resources as part of my reality. As Jesus said: " 'With men it is impossible, but with God all things are possible.' "[7]

The tentative, the hesitant, the fearful, the overly cautious, the

---

[6]Romans 4:20,21, KJV.
[7]Mark 10:27.

half-hearted, and the half-persuaded will never know miracle power. They will never experience success or victory in the visible or the invisible worlds. The goals they seek will always elude them, and they will never understand why. Never, at least, until they understand that their divided minds and spirits are actually projecting the seeds of failure into every situation.

The Time to Speak

When Mark told in his gospel of the cursing of the fig tree, he was careful to include the voice. Jesus *spoke* to the fig tree, and He told the disciples to *command* the mountain, which would do what they said if they didn't doubt in their hearts.

Scripture tells us further that Jesus stilled a storm by *speaking* to it,[8] raised three dead people by *speaking* to them,[9] cast out demons by *speaking* to them,[10] cleansed a leper by *speaking* to him,[11] and healed a Roman officer's servant by *speaking a word from a remote location.*[12]

Prayer for Jesus was communing with the Father, listening to the Father, watching the Father. What was the Father doing? What did He desire? Insight from the Father unified the heart and mind of the Son. Then, taking the authority that was His, the Son spoke the word of the Father. And the miracle happened.

So we see that miracles begin with certainty that God is present and that He has a purpose. Then we, His people, translate that purpose into the physical world by invoking His unlimited power. We do it with our mouths, speaking the word of the Lord

---

[8]See Mark 4:39.
[9]See Matthew 9:23–25; Luke 7:11–16; John 11:34.
[10]See Mark 9:25.
[11]See Matthew 8:3.
[12]See Matthew 8:13.

185

to the mountain, to the disease, to the storm, to the demons, to the finances that God wants to send to us.

We do not pray further, unless the situation specifically calls for prayer. In one instance, Jesus said, " 'This kind [of unclean spirit] cannot come out by anything but prayer.' "[13] That means we pray in those cases. Jesus also prayed at the tomb of Lazarus, but He made it plain that He was doing so for the people to recognize that God was performing the miracle. Then He Himself approached the tomb and uttered the words " 'Lazarus, come forth,' "[14] executing God's will by speaking.

Prayer is extremely important, and we are never to neglect it. Jesus gave us example after example, going off by Himself to pray, often for hours. And the Scripture writers are relentless in their admonitions to pray. Paul went so far as to tell us to pray without ceasing.[15]

But once God's will is disclosed, then is the time to shift to speaking.

Because of the great power the Lord has given to speech, it is terribly important that we Christians not use our mouths to speak slander, profanity, lust, or foolishness. The last point is delicate. We are not to think that the Lord lacks humor or that we should not have fun. It means merely that we should avoid jokes and foolishness about sacred things, for that comes dangerously close to violation of the third commandment: " 'You shall not take the name of the LORD your God in vain.' "[16]

Why would the Lord be so deeply concerned about our use of His name that He would include the issue in the Ten Commandments? He was giving us insight into the power of speech. We have in our mouths the power to kill or to make alive. We must not take it lightly.

---

[13]Mark 9:29.
[14]John 11:43.
[15]See 1 Thessalonians 5:17.
[16]Exodus 20:7

This significance explains why, on the Day of Pentecost when the power of the Holy Spirit came upon the disciples, an evidence of their anointing was their speaking in tongues.[17] Their voices were empowered by the Holy Spirit, a miracle that continues to be experienced by people of God today through what is known as the baptism of the Holy Spirit. From there, the disciples entered into ministry more miraculous than any they had known. They had been clothed with power from on high.[18] Their speech was a critical factor—again, not to be taken lightly.

The Major Hindrance

Having faith, seeing, refusing to doubt, speaking—all are critically important parts of the Law of Miracles. But Jesus made another point in the episode with the fig tree. Many people wish He hadn't.

"And whenever you stand praying, forgive, if you have anything against anyone; so that your Father also who is in heaven may forgive you your transgressions. But if you do not forgive, neither will your Father who is in heaven forgive your transgressions."[19]

With those few words, He set forth the major hindrance to the working of miracles in the visible world—the lack of forgiveness. Men and women, Christian and non-Christian, carry grudges. Any power of God within them is eaten up by resentment.

Is there any wonder that we see so little of the miraculous intervention of God in the affairs of the world?

We noted earlier that our initial view of God and our entrance into kingdom blessings depend on being born again and allowing the Lord to remove the cloud of sin between us and God. That

---

[17]See Acts 2:4.
[18]See Luke 24:49.
[19]Mark 11:25,26 (many manuscripts do not contain verse 26).

unobstructed view must continue if we are to evidence the miraculous. Being born again merely sets the process in motion; we must then walk step by step in a state of forgiveness. John the apostle said it this way: ". . . if we walk in the light as He Himself is in the light, we have fellowship with one another, and the blood of Jesus His Son [continuously] cleanses us from all sin."[20]

He went on to say that the one who hates his brother, who is not in a state of forgiveness with him, walks in the darkness and doesn't know where he's going. Thus walking in the light equates to living in proper relationships, which also means that we can be cleansed of our sins. The blood of Jesus does not cleanse in the dark or in a state of unforgiveness. Without forgiveness, our view of God and His kingdom is clouded. We will see no miracles.

In this matter, the Lord does not appear to be speaking of the loss of eternal salvation, for we have learned that this comes by grace through faith, not works. He is not saying a grudge will prevent you from ultimately going to heaven; He can be expected to deal with that at the proper time. Rather, He is declaring that if we want to experience now the miraculous power, say, of moving moutains, it is imperative that we live in a condition of forgiveness. Unforgiveness is not a characteristic acceptable in the kingdom of God. It contradicts the doctrine of forgiveness itself.

If all the law and all the prophets hang on loving God with the entire being and loving our neighbors as ourselves,[21] then unforgiveness can shatter everything. It reveals, among other things, the horrible sin of pride. For only the humble can forgive—those who surrender anger, feelings, and reputation to the will of God.

No Small Matter

We must see that these concerns are for our own good. Resentment, for example, eats into a person like cancer. Indeed, it often

---

[20]1 John 1:7.
[21]See Matthew 22:37–40.

causes sickness, both spiritual and physical, that can be debilitating and defy medical treatment. That is why the Lord dealt with the issue so many times.

One well-known dialogue occurred with Peter right after a bit of instruction on unity: "Then Peter came and said to Him, 'Lord, how often shall my brother sin against me and I forgive him? Up to seven times?' Jesus said to him, 'I do not say to you, up to seven times, but up to seventy times seven.'"[22]

Increasing the impact of the lesson, the Lord went on to tell a parable about a nobleman's slave who was forgiven a debt of $10 million after coming close to being sold along with his family on the slave market to recover the money. The man turned around and seized another slave who owed him $100 and had him thrown into prison for nonpayment. Here is how Jesus concluded the parable:

"Then summoning him [the first man], his lord said to him, 'You wicked slave, I forgave you all that debt because you entreated me. Should you not also have had mercy on your fellow slave, even as I had mercy on you?' And his lord, moved with anger, handed him over to the torturers until he should repay all that was owed him. So shall My heavenly Father also do to you, if each of you does not forgive his brother from your heart."[23]

It is no small matter, and I regret that the church through the years has not dealt more forcefully with it. As members of the kingdom, totally indebted to our loving heavenly Father, we must maintain an attitude and an atmosphere that promote harmony with our brothers. If we refuse to do that, we do not receive the blessings from our Father, and we block the flow of miraculous power.

Our principle weapon in the crises we face in the world is love, and love operates only in a state of forgiveness and reconciliation.

---

[22]Matthew 18:21,22.
[23]Matthew 18:32–35.

Pettiness must go, and jealousy and pride and lack of concern for others and neglect of the poor and needy.

A Friend's Illustration

I have a close friend, leader of one of the outstanding ministries in the world, who told me a story from his own life that reinforces the reality of the Law of Miracles as well as any I know.

At death, his father left him a fortune in property. In that period of grief and legal confusion, a family friend stepped in and legally, yet questionably, gained control of a part of the property.

My friend, when he realized what had happened, became angry and a seed of bitterness took root in him. A deep and churning resentment grew, worsening as he reflected on the nature of man that would allow him to take advantage of those who trusted him.

One day God showed my friend that if he was to continue in his ministry and to experience the miracles that had marked his walk with the Lord, he would have to deal with this resentment. He would have to forgive the man.

That was a difficult instruction from the Lord. The man was guilty. He had done something wrong to make money. Yet God said, "You must forgive him."

So, despite the spiritual struggle, my friend telephoned the man and arranged a meeting. I'm sure the man expected a confrontation and perhaps a shouting match; that's the way those things usually work out. But my friend, Spirit-filled and familiar with the purposes of God, followed through and said: "I want to ask your forgiveness. I've harbored resentment against you over what happened to the property. I've actually hated you. But I've been wrong and I've repented before God, and I totally forgive you for anything you may have done. And now I ask your forgiveness."

It was more than the man could stand. He began to weep, and the uniqueness of the moment broke him internally. Someone he had treated badly was actually asking him for forgiveness! It was upside down.

My friend immediately felt the flow of God's power in his own life. He was thoroughly free.

The two embraced and were reconciled.

In a matter of days, my friend received a call from an official of a corporation that owned a store on another piece of his property. The corporation had closed the store, and the future of the building and lease were unsettled. However, the official said, "You've been so nice to us that we're going to give you the store."

Again, things were upside down. That sort of thing simply was not done.

My friend, without lifting a finger, had overnight received a building worth far more than the piece of property that he had been denied in the previous episode. There was no quarreling or legal fighting. God had moved miraculously, once the roadblock of unforgiveness had been removed.

Futhermore, my friend's ministry, which centers on the miracle-working power of God, has flourished. Continuous forgiveness and continuous love—they are crucial in the Law of Miracles.

Miracles Are Available

If we would live in the kingdom of God today, by grace through faith, we would see far more miracles. We need only look at Paul's relatively compact, but nonetheless illuminating, instructions to the early Corinthian church to discover the miracle experiences that were considered normal.[24] He spoke of the

---

[24]See 1 Corinthians 12–14.

191

"manifestations" that the unblocked presence of the Holy Spirit within God's people would bring forth, declaring that these were for the "common good."[25] There was nothing elitist or abnormal about them.

For to one is given the *word of wisdom* through the Spirit, and to another the *word of knowledge* according to the same Spirit; to another *faith* by the same Spirit, and to another *gifts of healing* by the one Spirit, and to another the *effecting of miracles*, and to another *prophecy*, and to another the *distinguishing of spirits*, to another *various kinds of tongues*, and to another the *interpretation of tongues*.[26]

These are the supernatural evidences of God's favor and grace. They are among the effects of the blowing of the Spirit in our lives that the Lord was talking about with Nicodemus. You can't see the Spirit, which He likened to the wind; but you do see His effects.[27] When the wind blows, tree leaves move. When the Spirit blows other things move as well.

In my unending quest for wisdom, it turned out that the "word of wisdom" was a miracle of God that developed special meaning for me. All the gifts of the Spirit are exceedingly important when springing from faith, hope, and love; but the supernatural bestowal of the word of wisdom is to be cherished.

The word of wisdom, as I indicated in chapter five when talking about wisdom in a broader sense, is a glimpse into the future regarding a specific event or truth. It is an unveiling.

Many people think prophecy is futuristic, and it often is. But not always. Prophecy specifically is "forth-telling"—speaking forth the Word of God. Quite often it deals with the present, or perhaps even the past.

---

[25]1 Corinthians 12:8–10.
[26]1 Corinthians 12:8–10.
[27]See John 3:8.

I was praying one day in 1969, and the Lord spoke plainly to my inner man: "The stock market is going to crash."

This was startling, for I hadn't even been thinking about the stock market. Then He added, "Only the securities of your government will be safe."

In 1969 the stock market went to pieces and, in fact, has remained in a chaotic condition. It goes up and down, but there has been no increase in value.

That revelation has, I believe, application in the present, when a worldwide financial collapse seems imminent. It did not directly affect me or the ministry, but it was of great importance to the people of the country we were trying to reach with the gospel.

And the Lord has steadily increased this miraculous manifestation in my life and in ways more directly affecting the ministry than the performance of the stock market.

One day some years later, at a prayer meeting regarding an upcoming telethon in which we needed to raise the funds to meet the budget of our expanding outreach, the Lord spoke a word of wisdom as part of a prophecy. He responded to our concern about the burden we carried if we were to fulfill the mission He had given us.

I was speaking in prophecy about the presence of the Lord in what we were doing, and then the word of wisdom came regarding the telethon several days thence: "It will be so marvelous that you will not believe that it is happening. And yet this is going to happen before your eyes; and when it does happen, do not give credit to yourself, to your program people, to your computer operators, or to any of the things that you have done. But give Me credit because I am telling you now that I am going to do it. And when it's over, you will see it and you will know who did it."

Of course, the word was fulfilled and we dramatically exceeded our goal. He met our need and the need of the people we were ministering to.

193

And we could give no one else the credit. Despite the difficulty of the circumstances, we were in God's will, and He was with us. According to the pattern revealed by the prophet Isaiah, He had proclaimed the "new things" He was doing, even before they sprang forth.[28]

Probably the most frequent occurrence of the miraculous in my life has involved the word of knowledge, touching on physical or emotional healing or other interventions by the Lord in the lives of people. Such a word quite simply reveals information the natural mind would not know, about a condition or a circumstance in which God is acting. And there have been memorable times when, quite unwittingly on my part, the "word of knowledge" has actually been an unveiling of something that was to occur in the future—a "word of wisdom."

For example, a woman in California was watching the "700 Club" while sitting in a great deal of discomfort from a broken ankle encased in a cast. She heard me say on the air, "There's a woman in a cast. She has broken her ankle, and God is healing her."

The woman immediately knew, in a burst of faith in her spirit, that those words had been spoken for her. She rose from the chair, removed the cast, and, with increasing confidence, began to put weight on the broken foot and then to jump on it. The ankle bone had been healed.

The thing she did not know was that she had been watching a program taped a week earlier and shown in her area at that time. Further checking uncovered that I had actually spoken the words about her ankle before it had been broken. In a word of wisdom, I had spoken about something that was yet to occur.

The Lord has caused this to happen many times over the years in my ministry.

He wants each of us to reach up into the invisible world and

---

[28]See Isaiah 42:9.

allow Him to perform miracles through us in the visible world. He will do it without limits of time or circumstance. He waits for us to practice the principles He has set forth in Scripture.

The University Miracle

One of the most miraculous moves in my life, covering numerous laws of the kingdom and spanning an inordinate amount of time, involved the establishment of CBN University, a complex of graduate schools now underway at our Virginia Beach center.

I had wanted to buy five acres in the city of Virginia Beach, which was burgeoning, as a possible headquarters site; but the owner of the land I was interested in refused to sell a portion of the 143-acre tract.

But the situation changed the day I was sitting in the coffee shop of the Grand Hotel in Anaheim, California. Invited to a conference at the Melodyland Christian Center, I had arrived late for the opening luncheon and was eating alone. When my meal of cantaloupe and cottage cheese arrived, I bowed my head to say grace—and the Lord began to speak to me about the site three thousand miles away. People around me in the busy shop must have thought I was terribly grateful for that cantaloupe, for I remained in the posture of prayer for a long time.

"I want you to buy the land," the Lord said. "Buy it *all*," He said. "I want you to build a school there for My glory, as well as the headquarters building you need."

I had not thought of a school before. True, we desperately needed a headquarters building. But did we need 143 acres?

When I returned to Virginia, I called the banker holding the major mortgage on the property and told him I wanted to buy the entire site and build a school on it. "Praise the Lord!" he exclaimed.

I hadn't been able to get anywhere with my small thinking

195

about five acres, but suddenly I had acquired what God had directed—an interstate site worth $2.9 million, with nothing down, no principal payments for two years, and the balance at eight percent interest payable over twenty-three years. The terms could hardly have been more favorable! Furthermore, the Lord wasn't finished. He later gave us an adjoining site of 140 acres at prices that seemed miraculous.

The magnificent center standing on that property today is eloquent testimony to the power of God and the operation of the Law of Miracles. And, although I didn't know it at the time, the story had begun long before my California dialogue with the Lord. I eventually learned the following facts.

First, seven years before our acquisition of the site for the center, an Assembly of God minister had seen and shared with a friend of mine a vision of an international center on that same land. It would be a center reaching out to the world with the gospel. It would have students and dormitories, among other things, and would serve missionaries from around the world.

Second, at a point just ten miles from the site I had purchased, the first permanent English settlers in America had planted a cross on the sandy shore and claimed the land for God's glory and for the spread of the gospel. After 370 years, the ultramodern television facility with worldwide capabilities began to fulfill their dreams.

But that was not the only tie to those English settlers. I learned that a college had been part of their vision. Indeed, they had planned Henrico College as a school to teach the gospel and train young men and women for Christian service, hoping to reach the world through education. The plans for the college did not succeed. But the settlers believed the vision would last, as revealed in an introduction to a sermon pertaining to the overall settlement activity: "This work is of God and will therefore stand. It may be hindered, but it cannot be overthrown. . . ." They expected their descendants to rise to the challenge.

Interestingly, I am a descendant of the surgeon who came to Virginia in 1619 with the people who were to build Henrico College.

God had a plan. If miracles were required to fulfill it, then He performed miracles—all according to the laws of His kingdom.

FOURTEEN

THE LAW OF DOMINION

I was praying and fasting some years ago, seeking to understand God's purpose more fully. I heard His voice, level and conversational, "What do I desire for man?"

A bit surprised, I replied, "I don't know, Lord. You know."

"Look at Genesis, and you'll see," He said.

Genesis is one of the longest books in the Bible, but I opened it at the beginning. In a few moments I read this:

And God said, Let us make man in our image, after our likeness: and *let them have dominion* over the fish of the sea, and over the fowl of the air, and over the cattle, and over all the earth, and over every creeping thing that creepeth upon the earth. So God created man . . . .[1]

"Let them have dominion." My eyes went over it several times. Then I knew the Lord's purpose. He wanted man to have dominion—then and now.

---

[1]Genesis 1:26,27, KJV.

It was very clear. This was a kingdom law. God wants man to have authority over the earth. He wants him to rule the way he was created to rule.

You cannot help but juxtapose this desire of God with today's reality. The thousands of letters that pour into CBN, the pages of the newspapers, the screens of our television sets reveal anything but a people maintaining authority over their environment.

Christians especially show the symptoms of a defeated people. Many are sick, depressed, needy. They live in fear and confusion. Where, observers fairly ask, is the conquering army sung about in the great church hymns? Where is the blessing promised in the Bible from beginning to end? Was Jesus wrong when He said, "I will build my church; and the gates of hell shall not prevail against it"?[2]

No, Jesus was not wrong. Hell will *not* prevail. But we are seeing an Old Testament warning lived out among the people of God, and indeed all mankind: "My people perish for want of knowledge."[3] Men haven't been taught the Law of Dominion and the other principles of the kingdom. They are miserable.

But they can change immediately.

As in the Beginning

Almighty God wants us to recapture the dominion man held in the beginning. He has gone to great lengths to make that possible, sending His own Son as the second Adam to restore what was lost in Eden.

Remember, at the time of creation man exercised authority, under God's sovereignty, over everything. He was God's surrogate, His steward or regent.

The Genesis account uses two colorful words to describe this. One, *radah*, we translate "dominion." Man was to have domin-

---

[2]Matthew 16:18, KJV.
[3]Hosea 4:6, Jerusalem Bible.

ion. The word means to "rule over" or "tread down," as with grapes. It comes from a Hebrew root meaning "spread out" or "prostrate." The picture we get from it is one of all the creation spread out before man, whose dominion would extend wherever his feet trod.

The other word, *kabash*, is translated "subdue." Man was told to subdue the earth. The root means "to trample under foot," as one would do when washing dirty clothes. Therefore, in *kabash* we have in part the concept of separating good from evil by force.

With the first word, *radah*, God gives man the authority to govern all that is willing to be governed. With the second, *kabash*, He grants man authority over the untamed and the rebellious. In both instances, God gave man a sweeping and total mandate of dominion over this planet and everything in it.

But stewardship requires responsibility. And implicit in the grant was a requirement that man order the planet according to God's will and for God's purposes. This was a grant of freedom, not of license. As subsequent history proved, God's intention was that His world be governed and subdued by those who themselves were governed by God. But man, as we know, did not want to remain under God's sovereignty. He wanted to be *like God* without having anyone to tell him what to do.

The progression toward the Fall is enlightening. First, note that God, after giving man dominion over the fish, the fowl, the cattle, and all the earth, specified that this authority extended to "every creeping thing that creepeth upon the earth."[4] Man specifically had dominion over serpents.

Then, we ask, what happened when Eve was faced with a challenge by the serpent? She faltered and allowed the serpent to convince her that God's grant of sovereignty was faulty. She refused to exercise her authority, and, worse than that, the serpent took authority over her and manipulated her. Worse yet,

---

[4]Genesis 1:26, KJV.

with that first erosion, mankind allowed virtually all of his dominion to slip away.

It was the Law of Use in operation: Refuse to use what you have been given and you will lose it. Since that time, Satan has been exercising a type of dominion over human beings, deceiving them, destroying them.

God wants man to repossess that original dominion. He is ready to cause the Law of Use to work in our favor, if we will but begin to exercise what has been given.

We need to understand that God did not actually take the dominion away from man. He simply took away man's access to Him because of sin. Man still had dominion, but he lost the relationship and understanding necessary to exercise it properly. From there, the condition deteriorated as man voluntarily gave himself to the dominion of others.

As a result, man has for ages been neglecting and even misusing that which he was told to rule and subdue. He has, in effect, raped the creation rather than taken care of it. He has lost the humility and discipline to exercise dominion as God intended. He has exercised it arrogantly, or not at all. He hasn't been a servant of the creation—the animals, the oceans and rivers and streams, the forests, the mountains, the resources. He has violated the Law of Responsibility.

It is clear that God is saying, "I gave man dominion over the earth, but he lost it. Now I desire mature sons and daughters who will in My name exercise dominion over the earth and will subdue Satan, the unruly, and the rebellious. Take back my world from those who would loot it and abuse it. Rule as I would rule."

Application to the World

Included in God's grant of dominion to man was sovereignty over flowers, vegetables, and fruit. The mandate was all-inclusive: ". . . 'Behold, I have given you every plant yielding seed that is on the surface of all the earth, and every tree which has fruit yielding seed; it shall be food for you. . . .' "[5]

In one of the tragic ironies of all history, the Fall meant not only that man became a slave of Satan and his own base passions, but also that a sizable portion of mankind would become slaves of flowers, vegetables, and fruit. We have learned that those three can be cruel taskmasters. Last year in the United States, the tobacco plant caused the death of nearly 350,000 people, according to the Surgeon General. Corn, barley, rye, and grapes hold twenty million in alcoholic bondage. Together, these last four contribute to the death of 26,000 on our highways each year. But even that pales into insignificance compared with their fearful toll on human strength, creativity, and happiness.

Yet even more deadly is the hold that a weed, *cannabis*—called in Latin America "Mary Jane" or marijuana—has taken on the youth of our land, destroying their brains and their futures in exchange for a few moments of exhilaration. And we shudder at the fortunes that change hands and the crimes that are committed by those under the dominion of the seeds of the coca plants or the flowers of the opium poppy.

Last year in the United States, the cost of tobacco was $25 billion; alcohol $37 billion; marijuana $24 billion; and cocaine $35 billion. The cost of crime perpetrated by those addicted to heroin was at least $25 billion more. And well over half of America's staggering $250 billion medical bill can be attributed to illnesses induced by slavery to these items—vegetables, flowers, and fruit. Those statistics can reveal only a part of man's slavery. They are only illustrative of the financial toll we pay each year for our loss of dominion.

Yet attempts to set men free from this slavery are often met with derision and hostility. It does not matter that death and

[5]Genesis 1:29.

202

degradation are the outcome. Men outside the kingdom clutch their "pleasures" to their bosoms as if they were good, holy, and sacred rights.

You see, when man broke free of God's authority, he lost control of himself. Without a clear relationship with God, he became unable to see where he was going; and he soon became captive of what the Bible calls "the world, the flesh, and the devil." His own fears, his animal drives, his lusts, drove him. The devil, a malevolent power, played upon his base desires to seduce and entrap him. Then, as the human race grew, each man became a slave of mob psychology—the tyranny of the warped consensus of a sinful world.

Before the world can be freed from bondage, man must be made free from himself. This is why Jesus told the Jews of His day: ". . . 'If you abide in My word, then you are truly disciples of Mine; and you shall know the truth, and the truth shall make you free.'"[6]

Again, the writer of the letter to the Hebrews, speaking of the effect of the death of Jesus for mankind, said: ". . . that through death He might render powerless him who had the power of death, that is, the devil; and might deliver *those who through fear of death were subject to slavery all their lives*."[7]

When man, through Jesus, reasserts God's dominion over himself, then he is capable of reasserting his God-given dominion over everything else. That is the way everything on earth will be freed from the cycle of despair, cruelty, bondage, and death.

I furthermore believe the Lord would have man subdue the natural forces in the universe. Jesus, who was our example as well as our Redeemer, did this, as we have discussed in earlier chapters.

Without in any way advocating fanaticism, I believe God

---

[6]John 8:31,32.
[7]Hebrews 2:14,15.

would enable man, under His sovereignty, to deal successfully with the conditons that threaten the world with catastrophic earthquakes. Scripture makes plain that God uses natural disasters as judgment upon mankind; but I am convinced that were man to turn from his wicked ways and seek the Lord, he would be able to take dominion over the faults in the earth's structure and render them harmless. For the words of Jesus spoken to the tumultuous waters of Galilee still echo down through history with great power and authority: " 'Peace, be still.' "[8]

Similarly, man, taking his rightful place under God, would subdue the causes of drought and famine. World hunger would cease.

God's Fellow Workers

The concept of man's dominion over the created order is too much for us to comprehend unless we get a secure grip on the fact that the Lord thinks of us as fellow workers with Him in the development and operation of His kingdom.

Mark, in his gospel, tells how the disciples went out after Christ's ascension and "preached everywhere, while the Lord *worked with them.*"[9]

Paul, in his first letter to the Corinthians, reminded them that it was perfectly proper for both him and Apollos to be ministering to them. "We are God's *fellow workers* . . . ,"[10] he said.

Later, in a passage describing Christians as "ambassadors for Christ" to whom God has committed the message of reconciliation, he spoke of *"working together* with Him."[11]

---

[8]Mark 4:39, KJV.
[9]Mark 16:20.
[10]1 Corinthians 3:9.
[11]2 Corinthians 5:20, 6:1.

You see, the Bible's view is that God, in a mystery too great for us to fathom, has chosen to use men to carry the truth around the world. To accomplish this, He had to give them authority.

In addition, the Bible speaks of that time when God's kingdom and His Christ will visibly rule on earth. "If we endure," Paul wrote, pointing to the Law of Perseverance, "we shall also *reign with Him*."[12] That will involve exceptional authority. God wants us to prepare for it.

We see this exemplified in the accounts of the Lord's sending His disciples out to minister: "And He called the twelve together, and gave them *power* and *authority* over all the demons, and to heal diseases. And He sent them out to proclaim the kingdom of God, and to perform healing."[13]

Obviously, in the Lord's mind authority went hand in hand with the proclamation of the kingdom. Authority authenticated the kingdom. How would it be possible to say there was a kingdom of God that was to supplant the kingdom of Satan unless it carried power and authority?

Those two words, "power" and "authority," have a significance of their own, too. First, the passage says, the Lord gave them "power," which is translated from the Greek word *dunamis*. It means "resident power." Dynamite, for example, has that kind of power. Christians who have the Holy Spirit operating in their lives also have it. It is the power to perform miracles.

But the Lord also gave them "authority." This is translated from the Greek word *exousia*. It, too, carries with it the idea of force and power, specifically in the sense of authority like that of a magistrate or potentate.

Quite simply, Jesus gave them power to perform miracles and authority to use that power over the devil and all creation.

At another time, speaking to seventy people who had gone out

---

[12]2 Timothy 2:12.
[13]Luke 9:1,2.

to minister, Jesus said: " 'Behold, I have given you *authority* to tread upon serpents and scorpions, and *over all the power of the enemy.* . . .' "[14]

With that, He was referring directly back to the Fall, for serpents are a remembrance not only of the deception in the Garden of Eden, but also of the curse that followed. Serpents and men have been at enmity ever since God said the seed of Eve would one day bruise the head of the serpent,[15] pointing to the triumph of Christ over the devil and his works.

So, in giving his followers such authority, Jesus was indeed saying, "I reestablish your authority over the one who robbed you of it in the garden. You can reassert your dominion."

Our problem in the twentieth century, as we perish for lack of knowledge, is that it does us no good to have this authority if we don't exercise it correctly. And most of us don't.

Yet we have tried so hard in many cases to take seriously the words Jesus spoke to His people before ascending to heaven to sit at the right hand of His Father. We must examine those words closely and with understanding: "And Jesus came up and spoke to them, saying, *'All authority* has been given to Me in heaven and on earth. Go therefore. . . .' "[16]

Jesus had already " 'accomplished the work which Thou hast given Me to do.' "[17] He had destroyed "the works of the devil,"[18] which especially included the robbery performed in the Garden of Eden. He, the King of the kingdom, had "all authority."

"Therefore," He declared, "go!"

His people could move out to accomplish their worldwide task because He had restored man's dominion under God.

---

[14]Luke 10:19.
[15]See Genesis 3:15.
[16]Matthew 28:18,19.
[17]John 17:4.
[18]1 John 3:8.

Satan's Strategy

Satan, although defeated, is alive today, of course, and is as dangerous as we allow him to be. His primary weapon is deceit, and he uses it to prevent Christians from exercising the authority that is truly theirs in this world.

First, of course, he tries to entice us into sin, which can cloud or obstruct our view of the Lord and His will and, untended, can separate us from God.

He also tries to lead us into another form of sin, through unbelief. He tries to make us feel unworthy of the grace in which we stand. If he gets the upper hand in this, then we neglect the authority and the power given to us. They fall into disuse and, ultimately, vanish like the mist. The dominion that has been so awfully and awesomely won for us serves no purpose if it is not exercised.

We must combat this with all our strength and all our alertness. We must not be deceived.

We should recognize that we, in fact, *are* unworthy but that through the Lord Jesus we become worthy in the sight of God. We are sinners but, like Paul, who described himself as chief and foremost among sinners,[19] we "can do all things through Him who strengthens" us.[20]

Too many times, people fall into the devil's trap of believing that we can somehow earn our dominion. If we fall for that, we will never feel worthy, and we will never use the dominion given us. And we will never overcome the crises in the world.

If Satan can keep us in a state of timidity, discouragement, or embarrassment, he will nullify our authority and delay the man-

---

[19]See 1 Timothy 1:15.
[20]Philippians 4:13.

ifestation of the kingdom of God on earth. I have been amazed in recent years by the success of this very simple maneuver. He has rendered Christians ever so slightly embarrassed about being Christians. The world, for example, sees nothing wrong with a person carrying a copy of *Playboy* or *Penthouse* magazine around under his arm on the street, in the bus or subway. The same with a bottle of whiskey or a carton of cigarettes, with all of its life-threatening ingredients. Yet vast numbers of Christians have been intimidated about carrying a Bible on the street or bus or subway. They're afraid of being categorized as religious freaks, or perhaps old-fashioned and out-of-step with the world. They are nervous about being discovered in prayer or other attitudes perceived as different. As for authority—whether it be over Satan or over the natural order—their timidity is overwhelming.

And yet, as we have noted before, the Bible says, "God has not given us a spirit of timidity, but of power and love and discipline."[21]

Neither Satan nor the world has the authority or the power to do this to the Lord's people. They are flying directly in the face of God's desire. He wants us to assume our rightful authority and to hasten the coming of the kingdom on earth. Jesus emphasized this when He said: " 'And this *gospel of the kingdom* shall be preached in the whole world for a witness to all the nations, and then the end shall come.' "[22]

You see, there are many signs of the times that we can watch for, but this one is most critical. The gospel of the kingdom in all its fullness and power, with all its authority, is to be carried to every nation. Timidity must vanish. There will be "signs and wonders"[23]—miracles and other evidences of the kingdom.

---

[21]2 Timothy 1:7.
[22]Matthew 24:14.
[23]Romans 15:19.

The Law of Dominion, properly exercised, will guarantee that.

It Must Be Voiced

In practical terms, the Law of Dominion works much like the Law of Miracles. It depends on the spoken word. We are to take authority by voicing it, whether it involves the devil or any part of the creation.

We should not argue with Satan. We merely tell him that he has to go, that he has no authority, that he must release this person or that situation. Quite bluntly, we say, "In the name of Jesus, I command you to get out of here, Satan!"

Also, reaching the mind of the Lord, we tell the storm to quiet, the crops to flourish, the floodwater to recede, the attacking dog to stop. We simply speak the word aloud.

Again, the central point is to " 'have faith in God.' "[24] But we do not have to await a directive from Him in ordinary circumstances as to when to exercise the authority, assuming that we are walking in His will and yielded to His sovereignty. For He has already given us general guidelines: " 'Be fruitful and multiply, and fill the earth, and *subdue it;* and *rule* over the fish of the sea and over the birds of the sky, and over every living thing that moves on the earth.' "[25]

This especially covers "every creeping thing that creeps on the earth," symbolizing the one described in Christ's time as " 'the ruler of this world,' "[26] who has now been utterly defeated. Even though we still must struggle against those forces that willingly

---

[24]Mark 11:22.
[25]Genesis 1:28.
[26]John 12:31.

choose to ally themselves with Satan, that struggle has already been decided.

St. Paul described it this way: "For our struggle is not against flesh and blood, but against the rulers, against the powers, against the world forces of this darkness, against the spiritual forces of wickedness in the heavenly places."[27]

But since the authority for winning that struggle has been granted, St. Paul was confident that Christians will "stand firm" in "the evil day." The instrument for wielding that authority, he said, is the Word of God, which he described as the "sword of the Spirit."[28]

We simply are to speak forth our God-restored authority, preparing for an even more amazing era.

---

[27]Ephesians 6:12.
[28]Ephesians 6:13,17.

FIFTEEN

THE COMING KING

இஜ்ஃ Jesus said an astounding thing to His disciples: " '. . . To you it has been granted to know the mysteries of the kingdom of God. . . .' "[1]

Logic dictates that, if you are a disciple of His, you too have been permitted to know the mysteries of the kingdom. The reason is simple, but very important. He wants you to live in that realm right now, to master its principles so you will be ready for the new world order that appears to be rushing toward us. Why? Because you are to rule with Him in it,[2] and how can you rule if you aren't experienced in its laws?

If you are not a disciple, the mysteries are clouded, for flesh and blood cannot inherit the kingdom of God.[3] You must be born

---

[1]Luke 8:10.
[2]See 2 Timothy 2:12.
[3]See 1 Corinthians 15:50.

of the Spirit and receive access to that secret kingdom. That can occur this moment, merely by accepting Jesus into your life as your Lord and Savior. For God desires that you not miss out on anything; that is why He has been so patient these thousands of years.[4]

From the beginning of man's history, the Lord has been intent on establishing—through love, not fear—a kingdom of people who will voluntarily live under His sovereignty and enjoy His creation. That is the thrust of His entire revelation made in what we call the Holy Bible. He is building a kingdom. And a new, major step in that building shows signs of being at hand. The invisible world may be ready to emerge into full visibility.

One can almost hear Jesus speaking to His church: "Beloved, be ready. I have shown you the laws of my kingdom, the way things truly work. Use them. Live them. They will work for good even now."

There's a new world coming. And we already know its principles! There's the Law of Reciprocity, the Law of Use, the Law of Perseverance, the Law of Responsibility, the Law of Greatness, the Law of Unity, the Law of Miracles, and the Law of Dominion. There are others, perhaps not as sweeping, but nonetheless vital. Having been stated in the Scripture, they are God-breathed.[5] They will change the world as we know it and prepare the way for the new one, even speeding its arrival. They, and they alone, can calm the crises choking the world and thwart the imminent slide into chaos and dictatorship of the right or the left. They pose a realistic alternative.

The Outlook

Here is what we can expect to happen in the days, months, and years ahead.

---

[4]See 2 Peter 3:9.
[5]See 2 Timothy 3:16.

Having been regathered from the countries of the world, Israel, a unified nation living in relative security, will be invaded by a confederation from the north and the east. The prophet Ezekiel described this force as massive, coming like a storm, a cloud covering the land. He identified elements of it as "Gog of the land of Magog, the prince of Rosh, Meshech, and Tubal," joined by "Persia, Ethiopia, and Put," along with "Gomer," "Bethtogarmah from the remote parts of the north," and "many peoples."[6]

Various people have been viewed as Gog and Magog throughout history—the Goths, the Cretans, the Scythians—but indications are that this great power from the north may be the Soviet Union, for that nation occupies land specified by Ezekiel. Other present-day nations that we seem to identify in the confederation are Ethiopia, Iran as Persia, Somalia or Libya as Put, and Eastern Europe (probably Germany) as Gomer. It is noteworthy that Iran, at this writing, is mounting a crusade to "liberate" Jerusalem and is drawing near to the Soviet Union. Ethiopia is a Communist dictatorship; Libya tilts toward Moscow; and Somalia, although leaning toward the United States, has been Marxist. East Germany, a Soviet satellite, has positioned police forces in South Yemen and other parts of the Middle East. Thus, the various pieces of Ezekiel's prophecy appear to be easing into place.

When the forces move against Israel and its "unwalled villages"—"to capture spoil and to seize plunder"—it appears that questions will be raised by people identified as "Sheba, and Dedan, and the merchants of Tarshish, with all its villages [or young lions]."[7] Ezekiel did not say that these people would resist the invaders, but merely ask, "Why have you come here?"[8]

These questioners can probably be pinpointed as Yemen,

---

[6]See Ezekiel 38:2,6,7,9.
[7]Ezekiel 38:11,12.
[8]Ezekiel 38:13 (paraphrased.)

Saudi Arabia, and the United States, which was once settled by people who could be identified as Tarshish merchants. Tarshish was probably a Phoenician settlement in Spain, near Cadiz, that sent ships to Ireland, possibly to England, and then to the New World, their passengers traveling all over what was to become the United States. *If* there is a reference in the Bible to America, that would seem to be one.

Whether these questioners will assist Israel is unclear. Regardless, God, who is even in control of the invading horde from the north, will intervene in Israel's behalf with a great shaking—earthquakes, volcanic activity, fire, confusion, and even fighting among the allied invaders. He also speaks of fire falling upon Magog, the homeland of the leaders of the force, and upon "those who inhabit the coastlands in safety." This could, of course, be a vision of nuclear bombing. But it may also be the direct, miraculous intervention of God, for the prophecy says the following very pointedly: " 'And My holy name I shall make known in the midst of My people Israel; and I shall not let My holy name be profaned anymore. And *the nations will know that I am the Lord, the Holy One in Israel.* ' "[9]

According to Ezekiel, this will be followed by seven years of Israeli ascendance as the nation grows strong in the Middle East and increases in knowledge of the Lord, climaxed by a nationwide outpouring of the Holy Spirit.

Revelation's Clues

At the same time, the Book of Revelation appears to point to a successor kingdom to the Roman Empire that could roughly parallel the current European Economic Community.[10] It is a

---

[9]Ezekiel 39:6,7.
[10]See Revelation 17:9–14.

ten-nation confederation that has an eleventh nation added, along with a merger of two of the nations, apparently, and could be a forerunner of what is called the Antichrist. Presumably this group will make a league with Israel and then turn on her and begin to oppress her.

The leader of this confederation will be a spiritual being who will become a counterfeit Christ and draw men's allegiance. Exploiting confused, chaotic conditions, he will turn the league into a dictatorship, thus poising two kingdoms—the kingdom of God and the counterfeit kingdom—for climactic conflict.

Revelation points to another development that will be instrumental in this period. A system of buying and selling that utilizes individual marks will make possible the economic control of the world's population. The tremendous explosions in computer technology have made this feasible. Even now in Brussels, the headquarters city of the European Economic Community, a giant computer system—an interbank transfer computer—makes it possible to give every person in the world a number and allocate credits and debits on the basis of that number. It could be implanted in the skin by means of a chip or a laser tattoo in the forehead, perhaps concealed in the hair fringe, or on the hand.

Banks could institute debit cards, with the capacity to debit accounts instantly, and eliminate the need for exchange of currency. Even now, private business and government agencies are experimenting with so-called smart cards, which contain a tiny microchip computer capable of adjusting debit and credit balances as the cards are used. A next logical step would be the control of buying and selling through the embedment of such a microchip on the hand or the forehead, as indicated in Revelation.[11]

Thus, one scenario seems capable of fulfillment at almost any time: A major war erupts in the Middle East, with the Soviet

---

[11]Revelation 3:16,17.

Union leading a force into Israel. The force is destroyed. A catastrophic upheaval results, in which oil supplies to Europe and elsewhere are cut off. Europe is thrown into economic shambles, setting the stage for a strong-man dictator to move swiftly, with great charisma and verve, to establish a new economic order.

The Return of Jesus

In the meantime, the kingdom of God will move forward, its future never in doubt. Those who choose to live under its rule will do so and be continuously prepared for that time in history when Jesus Christ will return to earth. The Bible says He will come back to destroy this new economic leader and his "kingdom," setting up a reign of peace and justice forever.[12] The invisible kingdom will become a visible one. And the world—the principalities and powers, the angelic host—will see the way God intended for His universe and His society to function.

We need to understand that God will not abandon His world. He has from the beginning been concerned about the historic record and about His own justification. He does not act arbitrarily. It is as though He will send Jesus, then gather His archangels, the angels, the entire heavenly host and say, "Look, this is the way the world would have worked had man not sinned. This is what I desired."

God does not have to justify Himself. He merely does it because He is a God of love and order and justice.

But that will not be the end. It might almost be called a transition period, between the earth as it has been and the ultimate plan of God, in which evil and opposition to the Lord will be finally removed and paradise established.

The Bible says this transition period will cover a thousand

---

[12]See Revelation 19.

years, hence the name "millenium."[13] In it Christ will reign and there will be peace. He will hold everything together and His greatness will be manifest for all the world to see. He will be revealed in the fullness of what the Scripture has been proclaiming for centuries: He is altogether righteous and perfect; there is no failing in Him; His wisdom is absolute.

For a child will be born to us, a son will be given to us;
And the government will rest on His shoulders;
And His name will be called Wonderful Counselor, Mighty God,
Eternal Father, Prince of Peace.
There will be no end to the increase of His government or of peace,
On the throne of David and over his kingdom,
To establish it and to uphold it with justice and righteousness
From then on and forevermore.
The zeal of the LORD of hosts will accomplish this.[14]

Speculation will not be necessary. The beauty of the Lord will be evident to all, no longer dependent upon the vision of John:

And I saw heaven opened; and behold, a white horse, and He who sat upon it is called Faithful and True; and in righteousness He judges and wages war. And His eyes are a flame of fire, and upon His head are many diadems; and He has a name written upon Him which no one knows except Himself. And He is clothed with a robe dipped in blood; and His name is called The Word of God. And the armies which are in heaven, clothed in fine linen, white and clean, were following Him on white horses. And from His mouth comes a sharp sword, so that with it He may smite the nations; and He will rule them with a rod of iron; and He treads the wine press of the fierce wrath of God, the Almighty. And on His robe and on His thigh He has a name written, "King of Kings, and Lord of Lords."[15]

---

[13]See Revelation 20:2,4,7
[14]Isaiah 9:6,7.
[15]Revelation 19:11–16.

217

The laws of the kingdom will prevail, and His people will govern with Him. Food, water, and energy will be ample. No longer will trillions of dollars be spent on weaponry. It will go for parks and forests, for scientific advances as yet beyond imagination.

But, if His people are to govern with Him in these circumstances, they need answers to several big questions: How do you run a just government? How do you run a world? What principles work and what ones do not?

That's why Jesus talked so much about the kingdom. He let His apostles teach about the church. He, the King, talked about His own kingdom and the way it works. He wants us to master those principles so we will be able to serve with Him properly.

Remember, those who are great now will become the least, and those who are least will become great.[16] He will take the little people, His kingdom saints, and exalt them to positions of power. The wealthy, the arrogant, the oppressors—they will be diminished. Their authority will go to the saints, "the fullness of Him who fills all in all."[17]

The Removal of Evil

The Bible says that at the end of the transition period, Satan will be allowed to lead a revolt of those who have still refrained from voluntarily accepting the rule of Christ. Then, after a relatively short period, the Lord will remove Satan (all evil and opposition) and bring forth "a new heaven and a new earth,"[18] the ultimate and eternal kingdom.

---

[16]See Mark 10:31.
[17]Ephesians 1:23.
[18]Revelation 21:1.

Jesus spoke at some length about the removal of evil in a story that has come to be known as the parable of the tares.[19] It tells of a man who sowed good wheat seed in his field, but at night someone sowed tares—false wheat, weeds—in the same field. Both the wheat and the tares grew; and when the landowner was questioned, he said, " 'An enemy has done this!' "[20] But he wouldn't allow his workers to root up the tares for fear of what damage would be done to the wheat. "Let them both grow," he said, "and at the time of harvest I'll tell the reapers to put the wheat in the barn but to gather the tares for burning."

Later, when Jesus was alone with His disciples, they asked Him the meaning of the parable.

And He answered and said, "The one who sows the good seed is the Son of Man, and the field is the world; and as for the good seed, these are the sons of the kingdom; and the tares are the sons of the evil one; and the enemy who sowed them is the devil, and the harvest is the end of the age [the consummation]; and the reapers are angels. Therefore just as the tares are gathered up and burned with fire, so shall it be at the end of the age [the consummation]. The Son of Man will send forth His angels, and *they will gather out of His kingdom all stumbling blocks, and those who commit lawlessness,* and will cast them into the furnace of fire; in that place there shall be weeping and gnashing of teeth. Then the righteous will shine forth as the sun in the kingdom of their Father. . . ."[21]

Everything that is offensive will be removed from the kingdom of God, not by men or the church or military might, but by the angels. They will know the righteous from the evil, and they will know how to act.

At that point, the "sons of the kingdom" will be the only ones

---

[19]See Matthew 13:24–43.
[20]Matthew 13:28.
[21]See Matthew 13:37–43.

left, basking in the light of the Lord, living in ultimate reality and perfection.

Jesus reinforced this understanding for His disciples, following the parable of the tares with one about fish, for several of His close followers were fishermen. He compared the kingdom of heaven to a dragnet cast into the sea to gather fish of every kind. When it was hauled in, the good fish were sorted into containers, but the bad were thrown away. The explanation was the same as before: "So it will be at the end of the age [the consummation]; the angels shall come forth, and take out the wicked from among the righteous. . . ."[22]

At this moment, our minds can't comprehend the perfection that will exist then. We can't speak about it. Our ideas and words are still too limited.

But think of this: What would it be like if all the energies of men and all creation were founded 100 percent on love? Or consider it in reverse: What if there were not a single trace of hatred anywhere?

That is the world God created for us. No pride, no greed, no fear, no crime, no war, no disease, no hunger, no shortage.

The Final Step

The Bible speaks of a step in this progressive unfolding of God's perfect plan that would appear to come after all the other phases. It sets forth magnificently the unity and harmony of the Godhead and the ultimate unity and harmony of all creation.

The apostle Paul spoke of it in a complex passage on the sequences of the resurrection of the dead. The point we should see in our context is illuminated clearly:

---

[22]Matthew 13:49.

For as in Adam all die, so also in Christ all shall be made alive. But each in his own order: Christ the first fruits, after that those who are Christ's at His coming, *then comes the end, when He delivers up the kingdom to the God and Father,* when He has abolished all rule and all authority and power. For He must reign until He has put all His enemies under His feet. The last enemy that will be abolished is death. For He has put all things in subjection under His feet. But when He says, "All things are put in subjection," it is evident that He is excepted who put all things in subjection to Him. And when all things are subjected to Him, then the Son Himself also will be subjected to the One who subjected all things to Him, that God may be all in all.[23]

Again, these plans exceed our capacity for thought. Jesus, the Son and King, in whom all things will be summed up and united in the fullness of time,[24] will present all to His Father for all eternity.

What Will Men Do?

So, then, here we stand. What will men do?

Will they continue to ignore the principles governing the way the world works? Or will they learn from the secret kingdom?

I appeal to people everywhere to lay hold of the truths of our world—the Bible's insights into the way it works—and to put them into action. There is still time.

—Give and it will be given to you. This principle will not fail. We simply must begin to execute it—individuals, families, companies, nations. Imagine what our times would be like if we treated others the way we wanted to be treated.

—Take what you already have and put it to use. Don't wait

---

[23]1 Corinthians 15:22–28.
[24]Ephesians 1:9,10.

until you have everything you want. Use what you have. Multiply it exponentially, consistently, persistently. The wonders of the world will explode into fullness.

—Do not give up. Persevere. Endure. Keep on asking, keep on seeking, keep on knocking. The world will keep on responding.

—Be diligent to fulfill the responsibility required of you. If God and men have entrusted talent, possessions, money, or fame to you, they expect a certain level of performance. Don't let them down. If you do, you may lose everything.

—Resist society's inducements to success and greatness and dare to become a servant, even childlike. True leadership and greatness will follow. The one who serves will become the leader.

—Reject the dissension and negativism of the world. Choose harmony and unity at every level of life—unity centered on the will of God. Mankind flowing in unity will accomplish marvelous results in all endeavors.

—Be humble enough, yet bold enough, to expect and to do miracles fulfilling the purpose of the Lord. Once and for all, become aware of the power of your speech as you walk humbly and obediently. Most importantly, grasp and exercise the significance of the principle of forgiveness.

—As a follower of the Son of God, assume the authority, power, and dominion that God intends for men to exercise over the rest of creation. Recapture that which prevailed in the Garden of Eden before the Fall. Move with power and authority.

Obviously, there are additional laws of the kingdom that the Lord wants us to learn, and He will reveal them if we seek Him. But we can, and should—indeed, we must—begin to adhere to those that are now plain before us.

All is not lost. True, "the axe is already laid at the root of the trees,"[25] as John the Baptist warned nearly two thousand years

---

[25]Matthew 3:10.

ago, and those things running contrary to God's purpose will be cut down. The process has presumably already begun. God's plans will not be circumvented. Yet the movement to ultimate fulfillment need not be one of terror and agony. The crises of the world can be relieved. Just in themselves, the laws of the kingdom can accomplish that. The world can be a far better place as it moves toward fulfillment.

At some point, however, the laws by themselves will not be enough. A choice will have to be made regarding the kingdom itself. The laws will not operate forever outside the kingdom. Relief will only go so far. There will be a final shaking by God; only the kingdom will survive.[26]

So, why wait? Why separate the laws of the kingdom from allegiance to the King? Choose Him this moment. It can all be ours right now!

"Do not be afraid, little flock, for your Father has chosen gladly to give you the kingdom."[27]

---

[26]See Hebrews 12:25–29.
[27]Luke 12:32.